Sales and Operations Planning Standard System

With Reference Software

Other books by Chris Gray

The Right Choice. A Complete Guide to Evaluating, Selecting and Installing MRPII Software. Christopher Gray, John Wiley and Sons.

The MRPII Standard System. A Handbook for Manufacturing Software Survival. Darryl Landvater and Christopher Gray, John Wiley and Sons.

The MRPII Standard System Workbook. Darryl Landvater and Christopher Gray, John Wiley and Sons.

Sales and Operations Planning – Best Practices. John Dougherty and Christopher Gray, Trafford Publishing.

Sales and Operations Planning Standard System

With Reference Software

First in a Series on Manufacturing Software Standards

Christopher D. Gray

Gray Research

© Copyright 2007 Christopher D. Gray.
First printing: March 2007

All rights reserved. This book or parts thereof may not be reproduced in any form or by any means without written permission from the author except by a reviewer, who may quote brief passages in conjunction with a review.

Note for Librarians: A cataloguing record for this book is available from Library and Archives Canada at www.collectionscanada.ca/amicus/index-e.html
ISBN 1-4251-1542-X

Gray Research
181 Bunker Hill Avenue
Stratham NH 03885
1 603 778-9211

Chris Gray
Gray Research
1 603 778-9211
cgray@grayresearch.com

Printed in Victoria, BC, Canada. Printed on paper with minimum 30% recycled fibre. Trafford's print shop runs on "green energy" from solar, wind and other environmentally-friendly power sources.

Offices in Canada, USA, Ireland and UK

Book sales for North America and international:
Trafford Publishing, 6E–2333 Government St.,
Victoria, BC V8T 4P4 CANADA
phone 250 383 6864 (toll-free 1 888 232 4444)
fax 250 383 6804; email to orders@trafford.com
Book sales in Europe:
Trafford Publishing (UK) Limited, 9 Park End Street, 2nd Floor
Oxford, UK OX1 1HH UNITED KINGDOM
phone +44 (0)1865 722 113 (local rate 0845 230 9601)
facsimile +44 (0)1865 722 868; info.uk@trafford.com
Order online at:
trafford.com/07-0006

10 9 8 7 6 5 4 3 2

Table of Contents

Acknowledgements	i
Structure of the S&OP Standard System	vii
About "Standards" and this Series	ix
How to Use This Book	xi
From the Original Standard System "Structure and Limitations"	xv

PART 1: THE S&OP PROCESS

Chapter 1 – Overview: The S&OP Process	*1*

PART 2: CORE FUNCTIONALITY

Chapter 2 – S&OP Basics *Including Calculations and Reporting*	*17*
Chapter 3 – Additional Reporting Considerations	*33*
Chapter 4 – Additional Issues *Managing Change, Validation, and Linking*	*43*

PART 3: RELATED FUNCTIONS

Chapter 5 – Rough-Cut Planning	*57*
Chapter 6 – Feeding Financial Analysis	*65*
Chapter 7 – Measures of Performance	*75*

PART 4: GRAPHICAL DISPLAYS

Chapter 8 – Graphical Displays of S&OP Data   87

PART 5: SUMMARY

Chapter 9 – Functional Checklists   97

PART 6: REFERENCE SOFTWARE

Chapter 10 – Reference Software Overview and Quick Start   111

Chapter 11 – Reference Software UI and Functionality   119

APPENDICES

Appendix A – Accessing the Reference Formats   123

Appendix B – Accessing the Alternate Formats   125

Appendix C – S&OP Reading List   129

Appendix D – Software Disclaimer   131

INDEX   133

About the Author   137

Acknowledgements

I'd like to thank the following reviewers and contributors, some of the most talented and highly experienced professionals in this field. I am grateful for the time and effort they spent on this project, and for their contributions, both to the book and my understanding of how S&OP works in the real world. They were critical to the effort of improving the book.

Bill Belt
President
Bill Belt Excellence

Tom Buffo
Director, Advanced Manufacturing Applications
QAD, Inc.

Deborra Ciocys
Manufacturing and Business Support Manager
FUJIFILM Imaging Colorants, Inc.

John J. Civerolo
President
J. J. Civerolo, Inc., Partners for Excellence

Jack Gips
President
Jack Gips, Inc.

Phil Heenan
President
Phil Heenan Consulting

Bob Jones
President
Robert L. Jones, Inc.

Ron Kasoff
S&OP Manager
DuPont Teijin Films

ii The Sales and Operations Planning Standard System

Pam Lopker
Founder
QAD Inc.

Eileen Lucas
Chemical Industry Consultant
Formerly Commercial Operations Manager – US
Avecia Inc.

Matty Monheit
Senior Management Consultant
Metamorphosis Coaching and Consulting, Ltd.

Jim Prevatte
Chairman
Strategic Information Group

Michel Rabhi
Planning Manager
Coca-Cola Midi

Don Rice
President
D. R. Rice and Company, Partners for Excellence

Bob Sampson
mySAP SCM Senior Consultant
SAP America

Tom Wallace
President
T. F. Wallace and Company

Ken Weirman
Vice President, IT
Keystone Foods

I am especially indebted to two additional professionals who contributed both to the book and my own professional development over the years:

John Dougherty, with whom I wrote *Sales and Operations Planning – Best Practices,* gave me extensive feedback and recommendations on how to make the book better – both in terms of content and presentation. He went way beyond the call of duty in helping me with this book. He is a top professional and has made significant contributions to the field as a consultant, teacher, and writer and I have benefited from his suggestions, and from my association with him.

Darryl Landvater, my co-author on *The MRPII Standard System* and *The MRPII Standard System Workbook,* was generous of his writings and contributed a significant amount of material from the original Standard System to this effort. The introductory chapter *From the Original Standard System "Structure and Limitations"* is almost entirely his writing. . Some of his writing also appears in the S&OP basics, the rough-cut planning, and in the financial planning interfaces chapters. Darryl has a long history of contributions, including multiple books, video education materials, consulting and teaching, and software development, to manufacturing and distribution companies trying to improve their performance. As with John, I have benefited from my association with him over the years.

Thanks to you all!

Structure of the S&OP Standard System

The Sales and Operations Planning Standard System describes a simple set of software functions, primarily those in the areas of aggregate sales planning, aggregate supply[1] planning, aggregate inventory or backlog planning, reporting and display of key performance and planning information, rough-cut (capacity and material) planning, and financial planning. It describes the activities that are part of a working sales and operations planning process, as well as an explanation of the assumptions and the experience that led to these functions. In addition it describes some of the key interfaces that must exist with other essential company functions. For example, the S&OP Standard System describes the interfaces to resource planning functions like master production scheduling and sales planning, and the interfaces to lean manufacturing functions like takt time calculations.

The book is organized into the following chapters.

- The S&OP Process
- S&OP Basics Including Calculations and Reporting
- Additional Reporting Considerations
- Additional Issues – Managing Change, Validation, and Linking
- Rough-Cut Planning
- Feeding Financial Analysis
- Measures of Performance
- Graphical Displays of S&OP Data
- Functional Checklists
- Reference Software

One part of the S&OP Standard System is reserved for sample or reference software illustrating some of the concepts described in the text. The software

---

[1] Even though S&OP is increasingly being applied to situations where the production activities are completely or nearly completely outsourced, a high percentage of the number of S&OP users are still using it to plan their own production facilities. Rather than risk confusing the reader with a term that covers only one (although predominant) of the supply situations, I've chosen to use a term that seems to describe both outsourced supply and internal production: "supply planning". Consequently, throughout the book the term *supply planning* and *supply plan* will be used instead of *production planning, supply (production) planning, production plan,* or *supply (production) plan.*

included with the book demonstrates how these functions would typically be provided in an S&OP system, and can be modified and adapted to your own company.

Functions in the reference software include a simple menu system and reference formats for:

- Make-to-stock S&OP
- Make-to-order S&OP
- Finish-to-order S&OP
- Profit projections
- Cash flow projections
- Rough-cut capacity planning

The idea of providing the reference software is to help:

- Reduce some of the software design and programming effort required to build a company specific S&OP system.
- Evaluate and select commercial software.

The software was not designed as a complete system that could be implemented "out of the box", and doesn't have all the functionality described in the Standard System itself. What it does have are the most common functions and examples of how the core functions of S&OP should work. As a result, it could be used as the foundation upon which a full system is built.

Limits to the S&OP Standard

The Sales and Operations Planning Standard System covers S&OP and closely related topics like rough-cut planning, performance measurements, and financial integration. It explains the core functionality that must be present in S&OP software to truly call it S&OP. It is not all the functionality that might be part of a system – some companies may develop additional specialized functionality because of the nature of their markets, customers, regulatory environment, etc., but most companies trying to operate an effective S&OP system will need this core.[2]

The functions described here are limited to those required to support communication and decision-making focused on volume related issues. It does not attempt to describe all the key resource planning functionality of a modern ERP system (forecasting, demand management, master scheduling, detailed material and capacity planning, etc.) or the tactical activities involved in managing detailed supply and demand (sales management, customer management, materials management and supply chain management, etc). While these functions and activities are important to overall company performance, and are driven by the S&OP process, they are not S&OP per se and therefore are not described here.

Terminology[3]

Over the years, the term "sales and operations planning" has been used in a variety of ways:

- Some people use the term to describe the process of developing a forecast or sales plan, and improving the accuracy of that plan.

- Other people use it to mean a process whose primary focus is producing an aggregate supply or production plan (similar to the older term "production planning").

- Still others use it in an expanded sense to include the managing of both volume and mix, so that the processes of weekly item level forecasting, customer order management, and master scheduling are part of S&OP.

- Others would include all the tactical activities to manage demand and supply in the definition of S&OP if those tactical activities are triggered by the S&OP decision-making process. (S&OP by this definition might

---

[2] Companies implementing the concepts of lean manufacturing may have aligned their resources with the product families for S&OP and may not need much if anything in the way of rough-cut capacity planning, but may use rough-cut material planning to project their material requirements in lieu of detailed material planning.

[3] This discussion of terminology has been adapted from "Sales and Operations Planning – Best Practices" written with John Dougherty in 2006. See Appendix C for additional information about this book.

include elements of sales management, customer management, marketing promotion and pricing, supply chain management, and other similar activities.)

- Some consultants have coined new terms to describe what has been commonly known as S&OP. These include "Sales, Inventory, and Operations Planning (SIOP)", "Executive S&OP", "Enterprise S&OP", and "Integrated Business Management". There are probably others, and doubtless more will be added to the list in the future. While we're sympathetic to the intention of these consultants – trying to "unmuddy" the terminology waters – the unintended consequence of new terminology may be to add to the confusion over what S&OP is.

Throughout this book, the term "sales and operations planning – S&OP" will describe a **communication and decision-making process focusing on volume issues**. The intent of sales and operations planning is to get supply and demand in balance in aggregate, to develop a sensible strategy for dealing with mismatches in what the marketplace wants and what the supply chain can deliver (again in volume terms), to link the business' strategic planning and budgeting processes that are oriented towards the long term with the detailed and tactical day-to-day processes that handle mix issues, to ensure that both unit and financial plans are sensible and being met. S&OP engages key people across the company, as well as up and down the organizational hierarchy. Sales and operations planning is the key process needed to engage senior management so that they can see and influence the future results of the enterprise.

The terms *sales forecasting, demand management, customer order management, master scheduling* and *capacity planning* will be used to reference the related detail-level tools for the managing of mix. While closely related to S&OP, they are not part of S&OP itself.

The term *resource planning* is the umbrella used in the book to describe the complete set of planning activities that include both volume (S&OP) and mix (master scheduling, sales forecasting, demand management, material and capacity planning, etc.).

About "Standards" and the Manufacturing Software Standards Series

The idea for a series of books on standards for manufacturing software – encompassing the range of planning and execution functions in a modern manufacturing enterprise – has been rattling around in my head for a few years now. An earlier research report and subsequent book, called *"The MRPII Standard System"*, that I co-authored with Darryl Landvater was part of the inspiration, as were a series of other books that I've been fortunate enough to read – and profit from – during my career in working with manufacturing companies:

- In the early 1970's, IBM published as series of books "Communications Oriented Production Information and Control System" (widely known as "the COPICS manuals") documenting the concepts of an integrated manufacturing system. I was lucky enough to get copies of these books during my first job at Ohaus Scale where we were on the leading edge of small-company implementations of modern resource planning systems.

- In 1974, Joe Orlicky, the "father of MRP", wrote a book *"Material Requirements Planning"* describing, in great detail, the specific time phased material planning logic of MRP. Ollie Wight – one of Joe's personal friends and, while at IBM, one of his associates – joked that "besides Joe, only two other people have ever read his book" because of the detail covered in it. I must have been one of the two, and I benefited greatly from it.

- Later, I had the good fortune of working with Ollie and my friend Darryl Landvater in helping to define standards, based on the experience of working with companies to implement the concepts of MRPII, of what would today be called an ERP (enterprise resource planning) or Resource Planning system. These standards took the form of a research report – later a book, published as *The MRPII Standard System*. Largely because of Darryl's talents, the *Standard System* was the first explanation of the detailed logic of a working resource planning system that was both simple and in-depth enough to reduce the time in software design and development. Among all the works to that point that might help someone in developing the logic of an integrated manufacturing system, it was the first to be truly accessible to someone who didn't already know "how this stuff is supposed to work". It influenced an entire generation of software packages.

- A whole new world opened up for me when I read "*The Toyota Production System*" by Yasuhiro Monden. Professor Monden studied the mechanics of TPS and documented both the logic of the system and the practice of its use at Toyota. These concepts today form the basis for lean manufacturing and the visual execution systems that many enlightened manufacturing companies embrace.

Like Orlicky's book on MRP though, Monden's *Toyota Production System* is difficult reading, and may have had a smaller audience than it deserved simply because of how much detail it contains. It probably also does not benefit from being read in translation from its original Japanese.

But what seems clear to me is that most people could not pick up this book and easily understand the core calculations of TPS. As more and more American companies attempt to transition to lean production methods and want appropriate software to support them, developing this core functionality using Monden's study as a reference wouldn't be the best alternative.

And what was equally obvious was the fact that many companies were still struggling with both the overall design and the functional details of what a resource planning (ERP) system should really include. So this is an attempt to solve that problem, by taking each key activity of a modern manufacturing enterprise and describing the detailed functionality needed to support it as well as restating the essential principles of any good system design.

The *Sales and Operations Planning Standard System* is the first book in a series developed to solve this problem. The basic goal is to define the logic normally used in the planning and execution functions of a modern manufacturing system. The idea is to break down those functions into simple, accessible form by major functional area.

The Manufacturing Software Standards Series is envisioned as a series of books – initially sales and operations planning, then lean execution and visual management, forecasting and demand management, master production scheduling, etc. – with reference software to demonstrate how a typical software system would actually work. Each individual book will be about 100 pages explaining the basic logic of the function and another 50 or so pages explaining the associated reference software.

How to Use This Book

The book was designed for anyone involved in trying to design, implement, or operate an effective sales and operations planning process, and who wants to have effective tools to support it. If you work in IT with responsibilities in this area – are an S&OP process designer – are part of the implementation team for S&OP – or are one of the key users who are involved in maintaining, managing, evaluating and approving sales and operations plans – then this book is for you.

To assist you in building or buying an effective tool-set for S&OP, the first nine chapters provide a description of the process and the tools required. The next two chapters, chapters 10 – 11, and the first two appendices provide reference software demonstrating how the normal functions of S&OP are provided. All of the report and display examples from chapters 1 – 9 are included in the reference software, as are most of the basic calculations described in the book.

If you are building your own software – either in Excel or as part of your overall, self-developed system architecture – you may want to model your calculations around the reference software. If you are evaluating a commercially available software module – perhaps a module of your company's ERP system, or a reporting tool that provides basic S&OP comparisons, or one of the newer "simulation" systems that have both S&OP functionality and enhanced simulation tools – then you can use the reference software for just that: a basic point of comparison for the software functionality against the normal calculations and comparisons that make up S&OP.

Content
Functional Standard
Chapter 1 of the book provides a brief overview of the normal sales and operations planning process. It's a "refresher level" description of the process and was designed to establish the context in which effective S&OP tools operate.

If you are somewhat unfamiliar with S&OP – perhaps you've heard of it but have never implemented it before – you will need more detail on the process than what is provided here. To get to the level of detail needed to implement an effective S&OP process, you will probably need some additional education as well as some source material on the S&OP process.[4]

Chapters 2-4 describe the basic functionality of sales and operations planning in its most narrow sense: logic to develop and compare the sales and supply plans, calculations of inventory and backlog consequences, linkages to detailed forecasting and master scheduling systems, reporting and display considerations, etc.

Chapters 5 – 7 describe key related functionality – the minimum functions needed for rough-cut planning, for supporting financial planning processes, and for performance measurement.

Chapter 8 provides some guidelines for developing graphical, as opposed to tabular, or strictly numeric, displays of S&OP data.

Chapter 9 summarizes all the key points from the earlier chapters, and is a kind of functional checklist that a designer can use in developing a comprehensive system. Alternately, a software review team can use it as a basis for evaluating different software alternatives.

Reference Software
The Sales and Operations Planning Standard System includes access to basic S&OP software and spreadsheets matching the examples throughout the book. (See Chapter 10 about how to access this software). Chapters 10 – 11 and

---

[4] These three texts are particularly complementary to *The Sales and Operation Planning Standard System*:

> "Sales and Operations Planning. The How-to Handbook" by T. F. Wallace, second edition 2004. Tom's book is one of the best texts on this subject and lays out both how S&OP works and how to implement it.

> "Sales and Operations Planning – Best Practices" by John Dougherty and Christopher Gray. In this book, John and I describe the best practices of a baker's dozen excellent S&OP users.

> "The Sales and Operations Planning Handbook" by John Civerolo and Don Rice. 122 pages of samples, examples, specific step-by-step instructions, and internal audit data are provided to help your company start or improve your S&OP process.

See Appendix C for ordering information and additional source material references.

Appendices A and B describe the basic functions of this reference software, which was designed to help the reader understand how the typical calculations of S&OP, rough-cut capacity planning and S&OP-based financial projections are done using a familiar technology (MS Excel). These chapters were written to help you launch the software and get some hands-on experience using it. As such they are generally more of a reference for getting started than anything else.

This reference software includes various spreadsheet formats to show sales and operations plans, various financial projections of S&OP data, and rough-cut capacity plans. The spreadsheets used to generate the examples in chapters 1 – 9 are all included with the software so you can review and understand the calculations used. Because the reference software uses MS Access for database maintenance and MS Excel for its reporting functions, you don't need to be a computer expert to understand how the calculations are being done. If you've used Excel for business analysis, then you are probably more than qualified to understand the basic calculations embedded in the spreadsheets included in the reference software.

What to Read

If you are already knowledgeable about the S&OP process and have read either Tom Wallace's "How-to Handbook" or the "Best Practices" book that John Dougherty and I wrote, you can safely skip chapter 1.

If you are interested in how the functionality should work – which should be everyone reading the book – read chapters 2-9.

If you are a system designer (regardless of whether you are a technical IT person or a user) or developer, review the reference software and read enough of chapters 10 – 11 to get started with it.

From the Original Standard System "Structure and Limitations"

The key principles of a well-designed S&OP system are the same as those in any effective manufacturing system. As Darryl Landvater wrote in the introduction to the original Standard System:

> **Not an Ideal System**
> Although the Standard System describes the basic functions always needed …, it is not an ideal system with all the possible functions that could exist. Instead, the Standard System describes the simplest core set of tools and required system interfaces needed to make a system work. The Standard System is simple because simple is what works, and it is comprehensive because it covers all the areas that are needed.
>
> The definition of what constitutes a Standard System is based on the experiences of companies who have implemented … The experience of implementing and operating effective systems demonstrates that the fundamentals of planning, scheduling, and coordinating all the different functions within a manufacturing business are the same from company to company. This experience confirms that a standard set of tools exists to solve the problems of scheduling. These standard tools apply as well to a company making brassieres as it does to companies making jet engines.[5]
>
> So the Standard System tries to explain the subject of software clearly and in simple terms. Sadly, a smoke screen of technical jargon and a sea of acronyms in general often conceal computers, software, and data processing. The emphasis needs to be in another area. Clearly what is needed is a simple explanation of this necessary technical part of a manufacturing system. That's the explanation that follows.
>
> **Design Philosophies**
> There are a number of features that are a part of a good software package, but which are not specific functions. These are the design philosophies that have been embodied in the software. A designer who does not understand these philosophies will produce a package with limitations or fundamental flaws. Evidence that a software package does not recognize these design philosophies should be taken as a warning that the software may have

---

[5] For examples of companies in a variety of manufacturing and supply chain environments who have applied these concepts and principles to implement outstanding S&OP systems, see "Sales and Operations Planning – Best Practices", the 2006 book written with John Dougherty.

hidden flaws or limitations. The most important of these philosophies are the following:

Simulation of reality
(An MRPII) system has only one purpose: to accurately simulate the realities of a manufacturing environment. A software package that does not accurately simulate reality will not meet its primary objective and will not generate the kinds of results that are expected of it.

Consequently, the Standard System is not based on opinions of what "might work" or "should work." The only places where there can even be much opinion revolve around what people will accept. We have consistently emphasized people accountability in making a system work. This is where most systems, even those that are technically sound, too often fail.

Simplicity
All truly great things are simple, and systems are no exception. A software package needs a full set of functions. Any additional features in the system are both unnecessary and undesirable. They generally make the operation of the system overly complicated, and in doing so, destroy its native and inherent simplicity.

Responsibility
Systems do not make things happen, people do. Most things are accomplished because someone is directly responsible and can be held accountable for a task or decision. A software package should be designed to support the responsibility requirements for the day-to-day operation of the system. It should not obscure, impede, or try to assume these responsibilities. The people using the system should have direct operating control over the things for which they will be held accountable. Doing something because the computer said to do it is both lame and unjustifiable. A good software system should recognize the need to present what is happening to the people using the system. It should always provide the information for someone to explain why he or she has taken some kind of action and why that action makes sense.

Standardization
Standardization is general applicability. A system that adheres to the standards and conventions will be one that has fewer problems in implementation and operation. Standardization lays the groundwork for effective communications and problem solving. It allows the hard fought lessons of the past to be brought forward to today and into the future.

Noningenuity (Visibility to problems)
People have the ingenuity to solve the day-to-day operational problems when given a statement of the problem, visibility into the details of the problem, and a clear cut directive to solve it. A good system will point out problems and provide visibility into the issues and the range of solutions without attempting to devise a single solution, unless there is truly only one solution. By the time the logic and parameters are designed into a system for solving the endless

From the Original Standard System "Structure and Limitations" xvii

numbers of situations and occurrences, the system becomes too complicated and cumbersome. Even the designers are likely to wonder if the system will ever work. Instead, the system should allow the people using it to find a solution and then be able to implement the solution within the existing framework of the system.

What makes a package simple or complex? In whose eyes does a function provide for accountability or destroy it? Each issue can be seen as judgmental or subjective, and yet experience yields an objective basis for such determination.

Each point in the S&OP Standard System describes, from the point of view of a considerable amount of experience working with real successful users, what is simple versus complex, what maintains accountability and what doesn't, and so on.

PART 1:
THE S&OP PROCESS

The Sales and Operations Planning Standard System

Chapter 1
Overview: The S&OP Process

Overview and Objectives

Sales and operations planning is the key process for developing a company game plan. This game plan ensures that overall resource capability meets total market demand. While it is primarily a **volume-oriented** process, it does establish the set of numbers to which all other detailed plans and schedules can be synchronized. And it is linked to those numbers as changes occur in the marketplace, in the manufacturing environment, and in the overall supply chain. In this way it integrates all the functions of the business. In a very real sense it becomes "management's handle on the business" – the basic set of controls that senior management has to establish and adjust the activities of the organization in support of agreed business objectives.

A working S&OP process does all of the following:

- Institutionalizes management decision-making and communication, especially in the areas related to customer demand and manufacturing volumes.
- Balances demand and supply in a way that meets the needs of the customer as well as of the business itself and, where appropriate, provides for sensible shock absorbers when supply and demand are not equal.
- Integrates financial and operating plans.
- Links strategic plans with detailed plans and schedules.
- Regulates all detailed master schedules and sales plans.
- Provides "long range vision" to other more short sighted processes, especially to resolve potential long-range capacity, material and financial issues before they become crises.

First and foremost, sales and operations planning is a decision making and communications process. Instead of relying on decisions that may be made without complete information or by an informal communications network (that may or may not reliably disseminate them), a company that implements S&OP will use a structured process so that decisions about key business activities and issues are made using facts, and a communications structure where dissemination of those decisions is routine (institutionalized) and occurs on a regular schedule.

Sales and operations planning engages key people in sales and marketing, in engineering and product design, in manufacturing and purchasing and logistics, in finance and other key areas to ensure that all the members of the management team – up and down the organization – are working to the same set of numbers. And even more important, it ensures that those numbers were developed and agreed through a rational and integrated process that engaged all those key people.

Second, the S&OP process helps ensure that demand and supply are in balance over time, at least in volume terms, and in those instances when they are not, that there is a sensible shock-absorber in place to cushion the difference. Typical "shock-absorbers" for S&OP include *inventory*, the *order backlog*[6] (equivalent to the lead time for delivering against a customer order), or *flexibility in manufacturing or the supply chain*. In this way, customer demands can continue to be met, without passing highly variable demand into the upstream supply chain or immediately requiring that supply plans be adjusted.[7]

Third, it links operating plans with projected financial results, and tracks results against budgets and financial plans for the year. Although it's not exactly "a monthly update to the business plan" as it is sometimes described, it is the single process in most companies that is capable of showing performance against the business plan each month and projecting it through the end of the current fiscal year.

Fourth, it is the key linkage between the business and strategic planning process, and the detailed planning and execution systems in the company. It provides the mechanism to reconcile high-level plans, and then communicate the agreed upon company game plan to sales, finance, engineering, research and development,

---

[6] The backlog in a manufacturing company is the total quantity of sales orders waiting to be fulfilled. While some companies use the term backlog to mean "past due" orders, the correct definition encompasses all orders that have been booked but have not yet been shipped. An order promised twelve weeks into the future, for example, is part of the company backlog even though it is not past due.

For an interesting description of where this term originated, see American Word Origins, Houghton Mifflin and Company, or look it up on-line at answers.com.

[7] The fact that S&OP is a volume oriented process should not suggest that managing mix is unimportant. Nothing could be further from the truth – the fact is that you need to manage both mix and volume. Manage volume improperly and you'll never have the proper resources to deal with the mix – leading to poor customer service, lowered profitability, etc. Manage mix improperly and all the good plans you may have had for keeping demand and supply in balance in aggregate go out the window – probably leading to poor customer service, lowered profitability, etc.

manufacturing, purchasing, etc. An effectively managed sales and operations planning process promises greater visibility, better managed finished goods inventories or customer backlogs, and better customer service.

The approved sales and operations plan is a regulator of all the other plans and schedules: it is the budget that management sets for the master production schedule, and, in turn, all the supporting plans. The sales plan and the supply plan, two outputs from this process, regulate the detailed planning and scheduling for most of the company.

People are involved in developing the high level plans and reconciling them to create a company game plan. This company game plan, although perhaps not the best marketing plan, or the best manufacturing plan, or the best engineering plan, balances the needs of sales and marketing against the capabilities of the factory or supply chain to produce or procure. Individual sales plans can be created that are consistent with the factory's ability to produce. Conversely, supply plans can be developed to support both long-term sales plans and inventory and backlog targets and with the financial plans of the business.

In the long term, the marketplace should be the driver and the factory should meet the needs of the marketplace. In the short term, however, factory limitations may determine the rates of supply (production).

An effective sales and operations planning process:

- Sets objectives for customer service
- Projects the order backlog and customer lead time
- Projects inventories and finished goods inventory investments
- Establishes monthly shipping goals
- Establishes company manning levels
- Projects cash flows
- Projects profit
- Establishes budgets for material
- Drives capital investment decisions and expenditures

Finally, sales and operations planning gives distance vision to important processes like lean manufacturing, that would otherwise be incomplete with regard to long range material and capacity planning needs. While lean manufacturing ranks as one of the most important changes in Western manufacturing in the late 20th Century, it is arguably short-sighted, dealing with short term planning, and scheduling and execution activities – typically with a horizon of 8 weeks or less. There's no distance vision – no easy way to look 6 or 12 months into the future – and this is exactly what S&OP provides: a way to see capacity issues, volume increases or decreases, longer term financial issues before they become problems. Many lean manufacturers have found that S&OP and other long-planning activities are just what is needed to make their lean activities successful, because S&OP does what lean cannot: see out into the future.

The S&OP Process

To properly describe the S&OP Standard System, it is necessary to describe both the business processes that are part of an effective system as well as the calculations and displays that make up the software.

The S&OP process typically encompasses five major steps, involving middle management and others throughout the company who affect or are affected by demand and supply plans, inventory or backlog levels, internal or external capacity issues, financial results, etc. It culminates in an executive meeting to review recommendations, to decide among alternatives when there are unresolved issues from earlier steps, and to approve the company game plan.

The normal or typical five step S&OP process is pictured in Figure 1-1 below. In our experience, most successful implementers of S&OP use a process similar to this.[8] In cases where a company has varied from this model, generally speaking the modified process includes the normal five steps plus some minor modifications to accommodate company size or geography, organization and reporting relationships, or scope of operations.

---

[8] See "Sales and Operations Planning Best Practices", John Dougherty and Christopher Gray, Trafford Publishing, 2006

Figure 1-1

Five Step S&OP Process

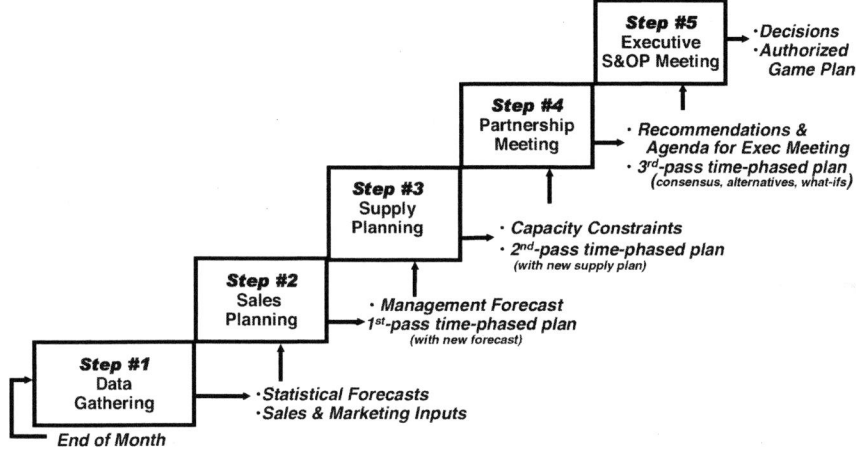

The "Five Step Process" typically includes activities for capturing past performance data (data gathering), sales planning, supply planning, a partnership meeting, and an executive review meeting.

Data Gathering and Review

Before new plans can be set or existing sales and operations plans adjusted, past performance needs to be known. Current positions against the sales plan, supply plan, inventory and/or backlog are needed to determine the best future plans for sales, supply and inventory or backlog.

Data gathering encompasses all the work necessary to collect performance data. Performance data needed for S&OP typically includes actuals against the plan, as well as other key performance indicators (KPI's). "Actuals" in this context means actual sales or bookings against the forecast, supply against the supply plan, actual inventory against the inventory plan, actual backlog against backlog plan. Key performance indicators reviewed during the S&OP process typically include customer service performance, forecast "accuracy", supply plan performance, master schedule performance, etc.

Most of the activity in "data gathering and review" is mechanical. The computer summarizes all the actual sales, actual supply, actual inventory, and actual backlog by product family or subfamily.

6 SALES AND OPERATIONS PLANNING STANDARD SYSTEM

Sales Planning

Sales (or demand) planning includes updating and agreeing on the forecasts and demand plans for future time periods, and recommendations regarding desired inventory levels and supporting supply volumes. The purpose of sales planning is to review *all* future demands and use them to arrive at a realistic, achievable and preliminary sales plan.

Considering that customer demands are typically beyond the direct control of the company (unlike manufacturing capability) and are typically highly variable, it is sometimes useful in developing the sales plan to develop high, low and most likely demand estimates. The high and low estimates can help in assessing what a reasonable response – in terms of inventory, backlog, capacity or manufacturing flexibility – may be.

Sales planning actually has two major phases, one of which has to do with standard products; the other has to do with new product introductions. However in each case, the basic objectives are the same: to get the best possible estimate of future demand and the assumptions that went into those estimates, to understand the variability or potential variability of the demand, to determine how much inventory or backlog is needed to absorb demand volatility, and from that to determine how much must be produced.

In some cases, the sales planning process for established products will run in parallel to the sales planning for new product development. Different groups may be responsible. In other cases, they will be done together and a single organization within the company will have the responsibility for the process.

The principal activities for each major product family or subfamily in the sales planning step include:

- Review past performance (last sales plan to actual) and measure demand variability.
- Evaluate and update assumptions associated with demand.
- Define future development needs.
- Validate new product development milestones.
- Develop or adjust the sales plan for future periods, in both units and dollars (pounds sterling, euros, real, yen, etc.). This includes extending the horizon so as to maintain a full eighteen months of future volume forecasts.
- Adjust inventory or backlog targets appropriate for absorbing demand variability when necessary.

- Project potential variations from the financial plan for future periods in dollars (pounds sterling, euros, real, yen, etc.) based on adjustments made in the current cycle.

The sales plan includes a forecast of total bookings for the product family. In the case of a product family that is make-to-stock, the sales plan is the statement of the anticipated quantity that will be booked and shipped from stock in the same period. In the case of the product family that is make-to-order, the sales plan is a statement of the anticipated quantity that will be booked in the period but shipped later. In each case, the sales plan represents the company's current and best estimate of customers' future requirements, often based on assumptions developed and reviewed in the sales planning process.

The sales planning process should have a way to record assumptions about demand for a family of products, and any agreed actions or assignments that have resulted from the demand review. Documenting assumptions is especially useful later when evaluating differences between planned demand and actual orders:

- Was the difference normal variability?
- Was the difference because of a major error in the assumptions – and if so what are the new assumptions?
- What happens to demand when assumptions change?

Formally documenting actions and assignments helps in defining who is responsible for which events or actions and for maintaining accountability for results. Who will do what and when? How will the results be measured? Subsequent performance reviews of the sales plan, or the S&OP in general, will typically also review the follow-through on planned actions.

Demand assumptions may record some anticipated market event or condition, the effect of a promotion during a specific period, the effects of introducing one product on another product, pipeline fills, customer plant shutdown, forward buying by the customer, entry or exit of a competitor, etc. Consequently, when an assumption is documented, the documentation should include either a start date (when will the effect be seen?) - or a date range (when will the effect begin and when will it end?).

Since the sales plan is an imperfect estimate of future demand, the desired inventory or backlog level may be adjusted as part of the sales planning activity. The estimate of desired inventory or backlog may be based on demand variability and desired service level based on weeks or months of sales, or some other management judgment, often based on considerations in the sales and marketing department.

As noted above, inventory or the order backlog then becomes the shock absorber for differences between the sales plan and the supply plan. Think of it this way - any time actual demand or supply are different from the plan, inventory (or the order backlog) acts as a shock absorber. Instead of having to instantly adjust supply to get back on plan, the inventory (backlog) can absorb the difference, at least for a short period of time. If demand is lower than expected, or supply is higher, inventory will go up (backlog will go down, lead time will get shorter). If demand is higher than anticipated or there's a problem with supply (such that supply is lower than planned), inventory will go down (backlog up, lead time longer). But customer orders can continue to be filled, and the factory can be somewhat insulated from surges or drops in supply simply because of differences in supply and demand. This also allows sensible decision making about how to bring supply and inventory back in balance over time, rather than making a potentially disruptive near term correction.

In this way, the supply plan may be set or held at a rate different from the sales plan. It may be set to build inventory in anticipation of a peak selling season. It may be set to reduce the backlog of customer orders as a way to gain a more competitive lead time. Or it may be set to increase the backlog on one product line to free resources for other product lines to capture market opportunities.

Once the sales plan has been updated and any adjustments made to desired inventory levels, preliminary supply volumes can be calculated and passed on to the supply planning process for review and evaluation. This is a mechanical step that occurs once any updates have been made to the sales plan for a family, but it is the first of several essential and related steps in the S&OP process – projecting the consequences of the new sales plan.

The simple math to perform the calculation of the supply plan from the updated sales plan and inventory objective is explained below in the calculations section of the S&OP Standard System. Suffice it to say though that required supply is the anticipated sales less any adjustments to inventory (based on planned inventory levels) or backlog.

In a perfect world, where the supply chain can respond as quickly as the market changes its ordering patterns, the supply plan would always equal the sales plan. But since this isn't always the case, the supply plan may differ from the sales plan by adjusting inventory or backlog up or down. In the same way (in a perfect world), the financial consequences of the S&OP would always equal the business plan. Since this isn't always the case either, sales and marketing people need visibility into the differences – good or bad – so that when necessary one of the plans can be adjusted or revised.

People from the sales and marketing departments, from customer service, and perhaps from a specialized sales planning function typically have the principal responsibility for updating these plans.

Supply Planning

In the supply planning phase of S&OP, the sourcing and supply plans are updated and developed. This includes reviewing the impact of required changes in the supply plans, and determining whether adequate resources will be available to support them. An agreed upon rate of supply for each product family is the second essential output from the sales and operations planning process. This rate, called the supply plan, is the rate of supply stated in gross terms. Depending upon the product, the rate many be 2,000 cars per week, 25 tons of dye or colorant per month, fifteen machines per month, etc.

The principal activities for each major product family or subfamily in the supply planning step include:

- Review past performance (last supply plan to actual production or supply)
- Evaluate and update assumptions associated with supply
- Evaluate the impact of the preliminary supply plan (developed from the updated sales plans in Step 2 Sales Planning) on the capacity plan for critical or key resources
- Adjust or specify a new supply plan that will support the agreed sales plan from Step 2 Sales Planning. This plan must be realistic in terms of capacity and supply chain responsiveness, and as such should be stated not calculated.
- Determine the projected impact on inventory or backlog.
- Project potential variations from the financial plan for future periods in dollars (pounds sterling, euros, real, yen, etc.) based on adjustments made in the current cycle.

The supply plan is usually stated as the rate per month for the type of product or a family of products. It is also possible to state it as a daily or weekly rate and convert it to the rate for the supply planning period. The supply plan is a rate of supply and does not include the timing or quantities of individual supply lots.

The principal factors that are used to develop the supply plan include the sales plan, supplier and capacity limitations, the responsiveness of the plant or suppliers, the current and desired inventory by period, and the current and desired backlog by period. Desired inventory may be expressed as a quantity, as days or weeks or months of supply. Desired backlog may be expressed in a similar way.

Just as in the case of the sales plan, the major factors, assignments and actions affecting supply will be documented as part of the assumptions built into the plan. In this way, when performance is not as expected, a review of the assumptions may provide some guidance into how the plan should be revised.

In a make-to-stock situation, the supply plan will be set using the beginning inventory and a management decision on the desired ending inventory for each future time period, and expected shipments coming from planned customer demand, customer orders already promised for future delivery, branch warehouse demands, and interplant orders is used to develop a supply rate. The resulting rate must then be checked against planned demonstrated capacity, as well as any supplier, capacity or material limitations. If it passes this check, then this supply plan is a candidate to be approved as the supply plan for the family.

The situation is similar in a make-to-order business. The supply plan is usually set using the beginning backlog of customer orders and a management decision on the desired backlog of customer orders at the end of the time period. This backlog information, together with the bookings plan, branch warehouse demands (if any), and interplant orders, is used to develop a supply rate for the family.

For a family of products that are a mix of make-to-stock and make-to-order, the supply rate will reflect the demand, adjustments to inventory, and adjustments to the order backlog.

Again the resulting supply rate must be checked against demonstrated capacity and any supplier, capacity, or material limitations before it can be approved as a supply plan. Normally this will be done as part of the rough-cut planning process. The two major parts to the rough-cut planning process – called rough-cut capacity planning and rough-cut material planning – are described in detail in Chapter 9 Rough-Cut Planning

In situations where the capacity or material limitations are based on supply levels, the supply plan can be extended by some manufacturing standard (pounds per unit, hours per hundred, units per unit produced) to get projected supplier, anticipated capacity or estimated material requirements.

There are other situations though where the key capacity (or material) limitations are not based on production, but are based on inventory levels, or the rate of anticipated bookings, or planned shipments. For example, in a beverage concentrate plant, the amount of cold storage warehouse space required is a function of the amount of finished goods inventory, not the production level. In a company making gas turbines to order, the amount of engineering capacity or engineering hours available may be a function of the complexity of the design job and the order booking rate (the work has to be done before the order will be placed). Similarly, in a company where some products are make-to-stock and others make-to-order, the amount of shipping labor required is a function of the shipments plan not the supply plan.

In all of these cases the projected supplier or engineering capacity, material or space requirements can be calculated in a similar way, just using the appropriate driver (inventory level or sales volume or shipments plan).

And as in the case of the proposed sales and operations plan coming out of sales planning, the effect of the proposed sales and operations plan on financial projections – and visibility into differences from the business plan or budget – is required. In some cases this might trigger adjustments to the sales and operations plan, and in other cases adjustments to the authorized budget itself[9].

People from operations, especially master scheduling, manufacturing, materials, and logistics, have the responsibility for Step 3, Supply Planning.

Partnership Meeting[10]
The "partnership meeting" provides the principal forum for reconciling differences between plans generated in the sales planning and the supply planning processes. From a practical perspective this means raising and resolving conflicts in how best to achieve a fundamental business objective:

---

[9] The way that supply is brought back into balance with demand, and the way that the volume S&OP plans are realigned with the business plan, and how fast this can happen is a function of the S&OP process assisted by written and agreed policies. For information about S&OP policies see Wallace "Sales and Operations Planning – The How-To Handbook, or Rice and Civerolo "Sales and Operations Planning Handbook".

[10] Some people prefer the terms Pre-S&OP meeting, Pre-meeting, Consensus meeting or even Compromise meeting for this essential step in the S&OP process. Regardless of which term you may use, be sure that this meeting is one of the most important steps in a working S&OP process.

balancing supply and demand over time. If what is best for sales and marketing is not reconciled with what is best for manufacturing with what is best for finance, etc., then each will have its own plan – and company performance will suffer.

The process of reconciling differences often this includes identifying alternative solutions where problems exist, identifying variances to the business plan (budget) and potential solutions, formulating agreed-upon recommendations to top management regarding critical changes to the plans, and identifying areas of disagreement where consensus has not been reached. Finally it's essential to communicate this information to top management with sufficient time for them to review it prior to the executive review meeting.

Here are the principal characteristics of the partnership meeting:

- Review sales and operations plan for each family, both in units and dollars (sterling, euros, etc.)
- Reconcile differences between plans generated in earlier steps
- Review the impact of the sales and operations plan on the rough-cut plans for critical resources and material
- Reconcile financial plans to business plans
- Where plans cannot be finalized, agree on issues and frame best alternatives – propose potential solutions to top management for resolution, with defined risks and costs
- Where possible finalize sales and operations plans

Just as the term "partnership" implies, this fourth step includes key people from functions representing demand (sales and marketing and customer service), supply (materials, purchasing, manufacturing, supply chain, distribution, logistics and shipping), finance and perhaps engineering, quality, HR, etc. with the overall objective of getting an agreement that cuts across the functional boundaries or silos of the company.

Executive S&OP meeting

Sales and operations plans from the partnership meeting are reviewed and a final S&OP approved at the executive meeting. The final approved plan is frequently – typically a very high percentage of the time – the plan that was agreed and forwarded from earlier steps in the process, but the executive meeting is not meant to be a "rubber stamp" of work done earlier in the process. There are occasions where the plan will be adjusted in the executive meeting. There are other occasions where the plan will be approved but with specific instructions to the supply or demand people in the organization to work on and adjust specific plans during the next planning cycle. However, the number of times where the plan is adjusted in the executive meeting tends to be small in companies with a working and effective S&OP process.

Principal characteristics of the final executive S&OP meeting include:

- Review key performance indicators and sales and operations plans for each major product family
- Review the impact of the current sales and operation plans against the agreed business plan (budget or annual operating plan)
- Resolve any issues forwarded from the partnership meeting, considering risks, costs, anticipated impact, and assumptions
- Where needed, make decisions necessary to approve or adjust the final sales and operations plans
- Document action plans and assignments

Sometimes the review process is done by reviewing aggregations of the data developed in the earlier steps, sometimes using graphical displays of the numeric data, sometimes reviewing the numerical data itself. Decisions and results from the executive meeting are published for the entire organization.

Normally the executive meeting is chaired by the CEO or the COO (chief operating officer) and attendees include all key executives as well as key individuals from earlier steps in the process. Generally speaking, there needs to be some continuity across the process. In smaller companies, where there may be few organizational levels and only a single master scheduler, the master scheduler may attend the executive meeting. In larger companies, the facilitator or "process owner" of the partnership meeting may attend the executive meeting to fill this role. As an example, in a company producing dyestuffs, the supply chain manager represents the partnership group in the executive meeting.

14 SALES AND OPERATIONS PLANNING STANDARD SYSTEM

PART 2:
CORE FUNCTIONALITY

16 Sales and Operations Planning Standard System

Chapter 2
S&OP Basics Including Calculations and Reporting

Sales and operations planning is an essential planning process that can be supported by computers and software. However, it is important to note that human judgment and decision making are crucial components of the process, and must not be "engineered out" of the system by the way the software has been designed.

Management is responsible for making the sales and operations plan the best estimate of future rates of supply. The value judgments and decisions needed to effectively handle the process of sales and operations planning cannot be made by a computer. The computer can only provide support, information and analysis, and simulations from which people will produce the final approved plans and schedules.

Because an effective S&OP process depends on evaluation and decision-making by knowledgeable humans, S&OP cannot be reduced entirely to numbers or software, no matter how sophisticated the computer software the system is built upon. Management is responsible for developing and then executing both the sales plans and the supply plans for the company, and they must have direct control over these plans. The computer should not automatically add to, delete from, or change the sales and operations plans once they have been developed and approved by people. The computer can critique and evaluate using some simple rules, produce simulations under a variety of scenarios, and produce recommendations, but people will be held accountable and therefore need direct operating control over these high level plans.

The sales and operations planning software explained in the S&OP Standard System provides people with information to use in developing and evaluating different sales and operations planning strategies. The software described here includes functions for evaluating, analyzing, and recommending alternatives. What it does not, and should not, do is automatically produce and approve the sales and operations plan.

Note that the actual practice of S&OP in industrial manufacturing and distribution suggests that most companies have comparable, if not identical, core processes and software. Companies using S&OP effectively typically have similar S&OP formats, have comparable policies for managing the sales and operations planning process, and meet frequently on a similar 'five step" cycle to review progress, analyze and evaluate proposed changes to the existing plan.

Most companies also use similar simple calculations to compare supply and demand, and to project the consequences of sales, supply, inventory and backlog decisions.

Basic Data

Any system that supports S&OP must provide a way to define product families and the supporting data needed for demand, shipments, supply, inventory and backlog planning, as well as the associated calculations to project the consequences of future sales and supply plans.

The basic data for S&OP is typically organized in the following way:

Families

As the explanation of the S&OP process suggests, sales and operations planning is typically based on product families or groupings, organized by either market characteristics or common manufacturing process, containing many different products or items. While it is tempting to think that S&OP could be done in more detail, say at the SKU or product ID level, the fact of the matter is that there are typically too many items or products for this to be workable. Grouping or categorizing items into families limits the number of groupings that have to be reviewed and approved by top management.

Equally important is the fact that the S&OP process is about planning volume, not mix. "How much manufacturing capacity, floor space, cold storage?" – "how much working capital will be tied up in inventory?" – "how many people need to be hired and trained?" – "how much profit will our plans generate and how does that compare to the budget?" – "how should we deploy or redeploy our resources to achieve the best results? – "what is happening in our marketplace?" - these are the important questions that S&OP needs to help answer. Diving into all the detail for individual items as part of the S&OP process will tend to divert attention away from these important volume related questions.

If the process is designed around individual items, the discussion will tend to revolve around individual schedules not the total volume that has to be supported. Only by elevating the discussion to the family level can management can see the real impact the plans it is approving.

The output of S&OP is an agreed rate of supply by family in some agreed unit of measure – it is not the schedules for individual items. The approved sales and operations plan for the family becomes the limit or budget used in maintaining individual schedules by item in the family.

A typical site doing S&OP may have between 2 and 20 families. As a general rule of thumb, most companies find that fifteen or fewer families are manageable, more than that may be unwieldy or difficult to manage. Or worse, by diving to too much detail, the process may degenerate to discussions of mix and not volume.

Family hierarchies

While it is normally best to limit the number of product families that have to be evaluated and maintained, there are several situations where more families are better than fewer families:

1. Where having more families communicates more effectively the requirements of the marketplace and the limitations of the factory or supply chain. For example, a manufacturer of fuel injectors may have as many as nine distinct product families, each forecasted individually, but may want to do supply planning based on five assembly lines.

2. Where the natural product line (marketing) families are not the same as the process (manufacturing) families, or where the natural families for planning in units are not the same as the financial families used for business planning and financial projections. For example, a manufacturer of lighting fixtures may have marketing families that are organized according to application, while the manufacturing process is based on fixture size. Or a large multinational corporation may have basic families organized by type of product regardless of where it is produced or sold, but individual businesses organized geographically (sales to North America, sales to the EU, sales to Asia Pacific, etc.).

3. Where it makes sense to plan in subfamily groupings, perhaps because of specific capacity constraints, but summarize for executive review and approval in more aggregate family or business oriented groups.

In situations where marketing and manufacturing families are not the same, some translations of sales, supply, and inventory or backlog data have to be made. Sometimes a planning bill of material is used to convert the product line sales plans (stated by marketing family) into plans by process grouping (manufacturing family)[11]. In some other situations, a sales family code and a supply family code can be assigned to each end item. This way, the planning bill of material can convert the sales plan for the family to forecasts by end item, and then the end item forecasts can be sorted and summarized into the appropriate supply family group[12]. In a similar way the supply plans can be converted back and forth between sales families and supply families.

The result is that the supply plan can be set within the constraints of key resources, suppliers, etc. This supply plan can be translated back, if necessary, to review the impact on the marketing family.

In situations where the early steps of the S&OP process are done using subfamilies and the later step or steps (especially the executive S&OP meeting) use families, functions must be provided to summarize the subfamily data into the family groups. The simplest way to do this is to assign a family code to each subfamily used in the demand or supply planning processes. This way the subfamilies can be sorted and aggregated to the correct families for executive review.

At the very least, the system should provide a way to summarize all the families into one overall grouping. As we'll see in the chapter on financial planning interfaces, this is particularly important when trying to see the overall impact of the sales and operations plan on the business plan.

Company Planning Calendar
Since S&OP is a process that plans forward from the current date, some kind of planning calendar is required to identify the start date of each S&OP period, the

---

[11] Planning bills of material for S&OP define the planning hierarchy and the relationship of each family, subfamily or item to the others in the hierarchy, expressed typically as a quantity or as a percentage. For example, in a case where one family is being "disaggregated", the planning bill might be defined as a parent (Family A) and three component families (Subfamily B at 20%, Subfamily C at 35%, and Subfamily D at 45%. Using these relationships the sales and operations plan for Family A can be disaggregated to Families B – D, or the sales and operations plans for B – D can be re-aggregated back to the plan for Family A.

Planning bills of material can define nearly any kind of planning relationship that is appropriate for S&OP.

[12] This also helps facilitate an S&OP process that can suit the needs of different organizational units in an extended supply chain: factories, regions, business units, etc.

number of calendar days in the period, the fiscal year to which the period belongs, etc. Normally the calendar links the S&OP process to the fiscal calendar (calendar months, 4-4-5, 13 fiscal periods, etc.) and also provides key sales and supply planning data like the number of sales days, number of supply days, production time in the period, etc.

As we'll see in the next chapter, the data in a planning calendar can be used to convert the sales plan to a rate of daily demand (sales), and to convert the supply plan to the rate of daily supply for each period. It can also be used to calculate takt time[13] – a key number for supporting lean manufacturing.

Basic Calculations in S&OP
Make-to-Stock and Make-to-Order S&OP Calculations

Two simple calculations help in managing the sales and operations planning process. In some cases, these calculations can be used to set the supply plan. More typically, they assist in comparing demand and supply so that people can decide whether to adjust the plans, and if so, by how much.

One formula, for products that are make-to-stock (MTS), relates supply to sales and the current and desired inventory. The other formula, for products that are make-to-order (MTO), relates supply to sales and the current and desired backlog. Both formulas are similar and are based on one basic relationship:

> Supply = sales + the adjustment in backlog or inventory

For sales and operations planning purposes, the two essential calculations that are based on this relationship are:

> Ending inventory = starting inventory − the sales plan + the supply plan
>
> Ending backlog = starting backlog + the sales plan − the supply plan.

---

[13] Takt time, arguably the most important number needed for implementing lean manufacturing, is an expression of the rate of production or supply that is perfectly aligned with the needs of customers. In other words, takt time indicates what the marketplace would like for output – one unit every X seconds or minutes – regardless of whether the supply process is currently capable of supporting it. Another number – operational takt time – expresses the rate of production that can be supported considering overtime, additional shifts, use of inventory, etc.

These basic calculations are "time phased" - applied to each period of the planning horizon to project the consequences of the sales and operations plan for the period.

Because the calculations are time phased, they provide a standardized way to project the results of management decisions. For example, by specifying the sales and supply plans for a period it is possible to calculate the inventory consequence for that period. On the other hand, if a management decision is to support a particular sales plan with a specific amount of inventory, it is possible to calculate the required supply in the period. (It should be pointed out that in situations where the calculations are done this way the numbers still need to be evaluated before the existing plan is adjusted. Simply being able to calculate a new supply plan does not mean that it is a do-able supply plan.)

Because the calculations that are part of S&OP are so simple, there are several realistic options for doing them. At the time of the writing of this book, most companies still use software running on their PCs – spreadsheet software like Microsoft Excel. Some companies use computer programs that are part of a larger ERP system architecture. A few use S&OP software from software companies who specialize solely in this area.

While there are a few companies, with few products and low volumes of data, who are capable of doing these calculations manually, few actually do it this way any more. The simple fact is that spreadsheet software is cheap and widely available, and most companies would see the minor expense paid off almost immediately in time saved by people involved in the S&OP process. Instead of "feeding data to the system", time can be spent in analysis and problem solving.

Mixed (MTS and MTO in the Same Family, and Finish-to-Order) S&OP Calculations

There are situations where both inventory and backlog exist for a family and where it is desirable to manage them simultaneously. For example, a company producing a range of electric motors might have a product family where some higher volume products are make-to-stock and others, sold to the same markets and produced on the same assembly lines but to a lower volume of demand, are make-to-order. In this situation, there will be a finished goods inventory of the make-to-stock products and a backlog of orders for the made-to order.[14]

Another situation might be in a company using a "postponement" or finish-to-order (FTO) strategy for order fulfillment. This would include any company finishing, packaging, assembling or filling to order after the customer order is received. For these situations, there will be an inventory of semi-finished inventory (perhaps a key component, primary option or base module, or bulk product) as well as a backlog of customer orders promised for future shipment, each of which will need to be planned and managed appropriately.

For these cases, the same basic kind of calculations described above – one relating supply to shipments and the other relating sales to shipments – are needed to see the consequences of S&OP plans and decisions. The two essential calculations needed to manage a family carrying both inventory and a backlog of orders promised into the future are:

> Ending inventory = starting inventory – the shipping plan + the supply plan
>
> Ending backlog = starting backlog + the sales plan – the shipping plan

As in the pure make-to-stock and make-to-order cases, these calculations are "time phased" – applied to each period of the planning horizon to project the inventory and backlog consequences of the sales and operations plan for the period.

Notice some subtle differences in the basic S&OP information depending on whether the family is mixed make-to-stock/make-to-order or finish-to-order:

---

[14] In most situations, it's simpler to separate the make-to-stock products from the make-to-order products and manage two separate families and aggregating to the totals. In this situation, the only "specialized" functionality required is the logic to summarize subfamilies into larger groupings and the ability to produce a display showing aggregated sales, shipments, supply, inventory and backlog.

However, some people prefer to manage a single "mixed" family where all the numbers are together and visible in a single display and where the basic calculations have been adjusted appropriately. This is the situation described here.

- For a mixed MTS/MTO family, all of the plans are related to activities for finished products in the family:

  The sales plan represents order bookings for finished products,

  The shipments plan represents planned shipments of finished products,

  The supply plan represents the plan to produce or procure finished products,

  The inventory plan represents finished goods inventory,

  The backlog plan represents the customer orders for finished products promised for future delivery.

- For a finish-to-order family, some plans are related to finished products, others to semi-finished products, and one relates to both:

  The sales plan represents order bookings for finished products,

  The shipments plan represents the finishing plan (taking semi-finished inventory out of stock and transforming it to finished product based on the customer specification) and the subsequent shipment of the finished product,

  The supply plan represents the plan to produce or procure semi-finished products,

  The inventory plan represents semi-finished inventory (a key component, major option or base module, bulk product),

  The backlog plan represents the customer orders for finished products promised for future delivery.

While the basic calculations for S&OP don't change much from the first situation to the second, there are some interesting implications with respect to rough-cut capacity planning. In the finish-to-order situation, supply for the semi-finished product has been separated from supply (synonymous with shipments) for the finished product. Since these supply plans may be running at different rates, some tools must exist in the rough-cut planning software to appropriately project capacity requirements for the finishing process based on the shipments plan, as well as for the primary manufacturing or supply processes being driven by the normal supply plan. These tools are discussed in Chapter 5, Rough-Cut Planning.

Basic S&OP Reporting

The sales and operations planning report displays the time phased sales and supply plans, and the essential calculations and comparisons so that the sales and operations planning process can be properly evaluated and managed. Factors that are part of the sales and planning process that can be represented as numbers should be displayed in this report. These factors include the sales plan, actual sales, the supply plan, actual supply, current and projected inventory, and the current and projected backlog.

Other factors - such as management decisions, assumptions about factors influencing the forecast, assumptions about flexibility and responsiveness, supplier, capacity, and material limitations, evaluation of past performance - are a different, more subjective type of information. They are typically tracked as part of the S&OP process, and they may also be displayed as part of the S&OP reports. However this subjective data typically takes the form of notes, remarks or annotations some of which may include hard numbers and others of which may be more like commentary.

Generally speaking, the sales and operations plan is most frequently shown in a horizontal time phased format, with historical data and future projections, in monthly time buckets. (Attempting to get to weekly detail in this volume related process is not recommended). Occasionally the sales and operations plan is shown in a vertical format, although most companies seem to prefer the horizontal display of the data.

All the time phased planning data for the sales and operations plan for each family should be shown in a single display or page – in other words a single display should show the sales plan, customer orders by promised date, supply plan, inventory or backlog plan for purposes of comparison. Scattering the planning data across multiple pages or displays is not recommended.

Hard numeric data shown on the sales and operations planning report typically includes historical information and future plans.

Performance measurement - on sales, supply, inventory and backlog - is a crucial part of sales and operations planning. Sales planning performance can be evaluated by comparing the sales plan against actual orders; supply planning performance can be evaluated by comparing the supply plan against the actual supply. Inventory performance compares actual inventory to planned inventory; backlog performance compares actual backlog to planned backlog.

Since inventory and backlog levels are a byproduct of performance to the sales plan and performance to the supply plan, in some sense they are reflective of overall company performance. If actual inventory is significantly different from the plan, it may be indicative of a big problem in sales or supply, or of a minor problem in each area that when added together create a much bigger problem in inventory – like underselling and oversupply (overproducing) in the same period, or overselling against the sales plan and undersupply.[15] The same is true of the backlog.

How Much History?

Most companies find it most effective to display at least three months of historical comparisons since less data provides little, if any, insight into trends. Some companies store and display six to twelve months of history, but three months is typically the minimum amount of history needed to operate an effective sales and operations planning process. In a seasonal business, even more visibility may be needed.

What Future Planning Horizon Is Appropriate?

Future operating plans normally go out beyond the current fiscal year. Anytime there are long cumulative lead times, the operating plan will extend beyond the end of the budget year. Near the end of the budget year, the operating plan will extend into the following year. Most companies find that a rolling horizon of eighteen months is the minimum visibility necessary to operate the sales and operations planning process effectively. The planning horizon is "rolling," because as time passes, new periods are added to the end of the horizon to extend it.

Although there are some companies operating sales and operations planning using a twelve month horizon, and others that have a horizon that flexes between a few months and one year (sometimes jokingly called an "accordion" horizon), neither is recommended. In both cases, the horizon is not sufficient to

---

[15] In some companies who have experienced poor performance in the past and who may have significant amounts of excess, aged, old style, or slow moving inventory, it is sometimes helpful to separate the saleable inventory from the slow moving. Future plans would be set based on the usable inventory. Financial projections would include the total of usable and slow moving.

support essential processes like annual budgeting and business planning. And if the horizon is not constant and longer than the capital approval cycle then some capacity issues may go undetected and unresolved even though they could have been dealt with easily had the horizon been longer.

How Is The S&OP Report Formatted?

The time phased data in the sales and operations planning report is as you might expect is typically displayed in three major categories – Sales, Supply, Inventory or Backlog - each of which will be separated into historical (past) periods and current/future periods. Typically three past periods will be shown, and eighteen current and future periods. These periods will nearly always be months, although far in the future some companies prefer to see quarterly periods. Weekly periods are not recommended.

The various parts to the S&OP report are discussed below:

Sales Plan

The section of the report containing sales data must include both the **sales (bookings) plan** and performance against it, and **customer orders promised for shipment** and performance against them. To handle a mixed MTS/MTO or finish-to-order family of products, planned shipments should also be included in the sales plan section of the S&OP display.

Planned bookings and the customer orders by promised ship dates are essential to the sales planning process and both must be monitored to have effective control over the sales plan.

The *sales plan* or *bookings plan* represents the rate of incoming orders. For a family of products that are make-to-stock – products that are produced in anticipation of an order – the bookings plan (the rate at which orders will be received) would typically be the same as the shipping plan. For this kind of family, the actual bookings would typically be the same as the promised shipments. But for a family of products that are make-to-order, the bookings plan is a forecast of the total quantity on future orders at the dates the orders are expected to be *received*, not the date that they are required and not the date that they will be shipped.

The bookings plan provides the early warning mechanism: by forecasting order bookings and then monitoring the actual orders written, visibility is provided at the earliest possible moment. Trends can be identified early and potentially out-of-control situations recognized while there is still time to take effective action.

If actual bookings in a period are less than anticipated, several alternatives may be available: marketing plans can be revised, promotional programs established, prices changed, new product introductions accelerated, and training for the sales force stepped up. If actual bookings are greater than anticipated, the impact on manufacturing can be identified in advance so that any necessary trade-offs can be discussed, such as increasing backlogs (or reducing inventory) versus capacity adjustments, working capital investment required to support additional sales, pricing adjustments, etc. In addition, sales can focus on protecting market position and share during a period of potentially scarce capacity.

The customer orders by promised ship dates yield visibility into future product shipments as well as anticipated revenue and projected cash flow. Existing customer orders provide good visibility into future shipments as well as a type of early warning signal. For example, if most of the customer orders are scheduled far in the future, the company may have problems hitting its shipping and cash goals over the next month or two – even though the booking plan is being met. By seeing the problem in advance, some alternative plans can be created to maintain shipments at the desired level.

The sales plan data section of the S&OP display also typically shows sales performance data – some simple comparisons based on the difference between the plan and the actual sales. For example, planned bookings can be compared to actual bookings, planned shipments to actual shipments. This comparison may be done by computing either the period-by-period deviation or the cumulative deviation from some specified starting point.

Graphical displays of the sales plan data are often helpful in identifying trends and problem situations. Characteristics of these displays of the numerical data are described in Chapter 9 "Graphical Displays of S&OP Data".

Supply Plan
The supply section of the S&OP display includes the authorized rate of supply and, for past periods, actual supply against this rate. The supply plan is the basis for allocating capacity, and a factor in the computations of inventory levels and order backlogs.

The supply data section of the S&OP display also typically shows supply performance data – again, some simple comparisons based on the difference between the plan and the actuals. Planned supply can be compared to actual supply, computing either the period-by-period deviation or the cumulative deviation from some specified starting point. A graphical display of these deviations is helpful in identifying problem situations, and as in the case of the sales data, graphical displays of the future supply plans are often helpful as well. For more detail on graphical displays of S&OP data, see chapter 8.

Inventory/Backlog Plan
The inventory or backlog section of the sales and operations planning report provides information to evaluate and manage the inventory and backlog for the product family. The inventory section shows past inventory performance as well as the planned stock build-up or depletion in the future. For each past period, the planned inventory can be compared to the actual inventory. For future periods, the planned inventory is calculated based on the supply plan and projected shipments, using the same formula explained earlier in this chapter. To refresh your memory of the formula used for a make-to-stock family[16]:

> Ending inventory = starting inventory minus sales plus supply.

The backlog section shows past performance against the backlog plan, as well as the planned backlog in the future. For each past period, the planned backlog can be compared to the actual backlog. For future periods, the planned backlog is calculated from the bookings plan and projected shipments, just as in the earlier make-to-order formula:

> Ending backlog = beginning backlog plus sales minus supply.

S&OP Time Phased Examples
Figures 2-1, 2-2, and 2-3 below are examples of the time phased planning projections[17]. Figure 2-1 is an example of one way to display the data for a

---

[16] As explained above, the correct formulas for mixed MTS/MTO families, or for families of products being finished to order are:

> Ending inventory = starting inventory − the shipping plan + the supply plan
>
> Ending backlog = starting backlog + the sales plan − the shipping plan

[17] Note that in most of the printed S&OP display examples in this book, the future horizon has been cut short – often to as few as four or five months. In a real working system, the future horizon would stretch out at least eighteen months into the future. Readers who are interested should refer to the reference software. It includes all the S&OP examples from the text of the book, with a full 18 month planning horizon.

make-to-stock family. Figure 2-2 is an example for a make-to-order family. Figure 2-3 is an example for a finish-to-order family.

In the next chapter, we'll discuss some of the additional considerations in designing effective S&OP displays.

Figure 2-1
Basic Time Phased Data in Make-to-Stock S&OP Format

Family	AXY			Type:		MTS		
Description	Large Widgets			Crit Time Fence		4 weeks		
Unit of Measure	EA x 100			Customer LT		2 days		
CALENDAR	History			Current		Next Year		
	AUG	SEP	OCT	NOV	DEC	JAN	FEB	MAR
SALES								
Current Sales Plan	1960	2268	2000	2002	2110	2345	2471	3171
Actual Sales	1680	1330	1950					
Difference	-280	-938	-50					
Cum Difference	988	50	0					
SHIPMENTS								
Customer Orders by Promised Date	1680	1330	1950					
Actual Shipments	1680	1330	1950					
SUPPLY								
Current Supply Plan	1960	2268	2000	1750	1750	2100	2800	3150
Actual Supply	2100	1470	2100					
Difference	140	-798	100					
Cum Difference	560	-238	-138					
INVENTORY								
Current Inventory Plan		2240	2660	2800	2698	2338	2093	2422	2401
Actual	2240	2660	2800	2950					
Difference		420	140	150					

Also note that, generally speaking, the S&OP examples shown in the book are generated from one of three basic spreadsheets (one for make-to-stock, another for make-to-order, another for finish-to-order). In order to reduce the amount of information being introduced "all at once" or before the topic is introduced in the book itself, rows have been hidden prior to generating the figure in the book. You can see the complete spreadsheet, with no hidden data, by opening the reference software that is available with the book. See Chapter 10.

Figure 2-2
Make-to-Order S&OP Format

Family	**BHK**	**Type**	**MTS**
Description	**Large Pumps**	**Critical Time Fence**	**10 weeks**
Unit of Measure	**EACH X 100**	**Cust Lead Time**	**12 weeks**

CALENDAR		**History**			**Current**		**Next Year**		
		AUG	**SEP**	**OCT**	**NOV**	**DEC**	**JAN**	**FEB**	**MAR**
SALES									
Current Sales Plan		**1470**	**1890**	**1820**	**1820**	**1400**	**1400**	**1400**	**1540**
Actual Sales		**1400**	**1645**	**1750**					
Difference		**-70**	**-245**	**-70**					
SHIPMENTS									
Customer Orders by Promised Date		**1470**	**1890**	**1820**	**1820**	**1470**	**1540**	**280**	**0**
Actual Shipments		**1456**	**1890**	**1820**					
SUPPLY									
Current Supply Plan		**1470**	**1890**	**1820**	**1820**	**1470**	**1540**	**1540**	**1540**
Actual Supply		**1456**	**1890**	**1820**					
Difference		**-14**	**14**	**0**					
BACKLOG									
Current Backlog Plan		**5481**	**5425**	**5180**	**5110**	**5040**	**4900**	**4760**	**4760**
Actual	**5481**	**5425**	**5180**	**5110**					
Difference		**-56**	**-245**	**-70**					

Figure 2-3
Finish-to-Order (Postponement) S&OP Format

Family	BHK	Type	FTO
Description	Large Pumps	Critical Time Fence	10 weeks
Unit of Measure	EACH X 100	Cust Lead Time	12 weeks

CALENDAR	History			Current		Next Year		
	AUG	SEP	OCT	NOV	DEC	JAN	FEB	MAR
SALES								
Current Sales Plan	1470	1890	1820	1820	1400	1400	1400	1540
Actual Sales	1400	1645	1750					
Difference	-70	-245	-70					
FINISHING AND SHIPMENTS (Finished Product)								
Current Shipments Plan	1470	1890	1820	1820	1470	1400	1400	1540
Customer Orders by Promised Date	1470	1890	1820	1820	0			
Actual Shipments	1470	1890	1820					
SUPPLY (Semi-finished material)								
Current Supply Plan	1470	1890	1820	1820	1470	1540	1540	1540
Actual Supply	1456	1904	1820					
Difference	-14	14	0					
SEMI-FINISHED INVENTORY								
Current Inventory Plan	1750	1736	1750	1750	1750	1890	2030	2030
Actual	1750 1736	1750	1750					
Difference	-14	14	0					
BACKLOG								
Current Backlog Plan	2205	2135	1890	1820	1750	1750	1750	1750
Actual	2205 2135	1890	1820					
Difference	-70	-245	-70					

Chapter 3
Additional Reporting Considerations

Additional Data

The sales and operations planning report should also include additional information about the family and the S&OP data. This additional information includes data in both units and dollars. The dollar oriented data will be discussed specifically in Chapter 6 Feeding Financial Analysis. Unit oriented information includes:

1. Descriptive information
2. Additional time phased data
    - Business plan
    - Year-to-date (YTD) performance
      Sales versus business plan
      Actual sales to date
      Actual shipments to date
      Actual supply to date
    - Projected performance through to the end of the year
      Projected business plan performance
      Projected sales plan performance
      Projected shipments performance
      Projected supply performance
      Projected ending inventory
      Projected ending backlog
    - Prior sales and supply plans to provide visibility to change over time
    - Inventory and backlog targets
    - Inventory turnover and backlog in weeks
3. Commentary
    - Analysis of past performance (sales, supply, inventory and backlog)
    - Assumptions about future plans (demand and supply)
    - New product development status

Descriptive Information

Descriptive information showing family identification and key planning parameters should be shown along with the time phased information. Any family data that affects the calculations and comparisons must be shown.

Additional Time Phased Data

The S&OP display should provide visibility into the agreed business plan and performance tracking against it. Generally speaking this means that the agreed business plan should be displayed along with the other time phased data, and columns added for year-to-date actual performance (actual sales year-to-date, actual production year-to-date) and projected performance. Projected performance reflects actuals-to-date plus current plans into the future.

The cumulative impact of actual performance to date is particularly helpful since it is the most accurate reflection of what is happening with sales in light of actual unit performance, and is perhaps the best validation of the plans in place through the end of the current fiscal year. (In many companies, the cum totals are based on current year performance and reset at the end of the fiscal year. Other companies prefer to specify when or how frequently they are reset, so that cum totals can be carried across fiscal years. The theory here is that arbitrarily resetting at year end may cause lost visibility to cumulative performance in the very recent past.)

Where there are differences between the projections from sales and operations plan and the business plan, there are several alternatives: revise S&OP to meet the business plan, revise the business plan to reflect current conditions as reflected in S&OP, or understand the variance between the original operating plan and the S&OP without revising either.

Sometimes the projected performance against one family will be running ahead of the business plan for the family, while the projected performance against another family will be running behind the business plan – so that overall the company performance is on or close to on-target. This would be an instance where the business plans for the individual families probably wouldn't be changed.

In other cases where the business plan is not being met, it may not be possible to change either the business plan or the S&OP right now, and further analysis may be required. Regardless of what action is taken now or in the future though, it is essential to understand and agree to the impact of a sales and operations plan that is different from the business plan, and continue to look for ways to bring them in line.

Figure 3-1 is an example of how the business plan (annual operating plan) and sales plan data might appear when current performance and expected results are shown. Notice in particular the section labeled *ANNUAL OPERATING PLAN* and the columns *Cum, Year-to-Date* and *Current Year*.

Refer to Chapter 10 for information about accessing the full time phased display.

Figure 3-1
Current Performance and Expected Results (Units)

CALENDAR		History			Year-to-Date	Current		Current Year	Next Year		
		AUG	SEP	OCT	Planned	NOV	DEC	Planned	JAN	FEB	MAR
ANNUAL OPERATING PLAN	CUM				Year-to-Date YTD Results			Current Year Expected Results			
Budgeted Sales	14300	2000	2300	2100	20700	2100	2200	25000	2345	2471	3171
Perf to Budget	17440	1680	1330	1950	22400	2002	2110	26512			
Cum Diff Perf to Budget	3140	2820	1850	1700	1700	1602	1512	1512			
SALES	CUM				YTD Results			Expected Results			
Current Sales Plan	16172	1960	2268	2000	22400	2002	2110	26512	2345	2471	3171
Actual Sales	17440	1680	1330	1950	22400						
Difference	1268	-280	-938	-50							
Cum Difference	1268	988	50	0							
SHIPMENTS	CUM				YTD Results			Expected Results			
Customer Orders by Promised Date	17440	1680	1330	1950	22400			26512			
Actual Shipments	17440	1680	1330	1950	22400						
SUPPLY	CUM				YTD Results			Expected Results			
Current Supply Plan	12110	1960	2268	2000	18338	1750	1750	21700	2100	2800	3150
Actual Supply	12530	2100	1470	2100	18200						
Difference	420	140	-798	100	-138						
Cum Difference	420	560	-238	-138	-138						
INVENTORY											
Current Inventory Plan	3088	2240	2660	2800	2950	2698	2338	2338	2093	2422	2401
Actual	2240	2660	2800	2950	2950						
Difference	-848	420	140	150	150						

Visibility into Prior Plans

Frequently it is helpful to see how the sales and operations plan has changed over time. Some companies retain previous versions of the plan and either display it as part of the other S&OP data or make it available on demand.

An example of how "prior plan" or "last plan" data might be displayed in the time phased report is shown in Figure 3-2. Notice specifically the *Last Sales Plan, Last Supply Plan* and *Last Inventory Plan* data in the example below. The numbers shown in any given past period reflect the last plan in place prior to getting actuals (sales, supply and inventory) for that period. Also notice the design choice to set the Current Plan for any past periods to the actual performance for the period. (This design choice would allow the Actual line in each section of the display to be removed entirely).

36 SALES AND OPERATIONS PLANNING STANDARD SYSTEM

Figure 3-2
Prior Plans Data

CALENDAR	CUM	History AUG	History SEP	OCT	Year-to-Date Planned	Current NOV	Current DEC	Current Year Planned	Next Year JAN	FEB	MAR
ANNUAL OPERATING PLAN					Year-to-Date YTD Results			Current Year Expected Results			
Budgeted Sales	14300	2000	2300	2100	20700	2100	2200	25000	2345	2471	3171
Perf to Budget	17440	1680	1330	1950	22400	2002	2110	26512			
Cum Diff Perf to Budget	3140	2820	1850	1700	1700	1602	1512	1512			
SALES	CUM				YTD Results			Expected Results			
Last Sales Plan	16172	1960	2268	2000	22400	2100	2200	26700	2400	2500	3200
Current Sales Plan	17440	1680	1330	1950	22400	2002	2110	26512	2345	2471	3171
Actual Sales	17440	1680	1330	1950	22400						
Difference	1268	-280	-938	-50							
Cum Difference	1268	988	50	0							
SHIPMENTS	CUM				YTD Results			Expected Results			
Customer Orders by Promised Date	17440	1680	1330	1950	22400			26512			
Actual Shipments	17440	1680	1330	1950	22400						
SUPPLY	CUM				YTD Results			Expected Results			
Last Supply Plan	12110	1960	2268	2000	18338	1750	1800	21888	2150	2850	3150
Current Supply Plan	12530	2100	1470	2100	18200	1750	1750	21700	2100	2800	3150
Actual Supply	12530	2100	1470	2100	18200						
Difference	420	140	-798	100	-138						
Cum Difference	420	560	-238	-138	-138						
					YTD Results			Expected Results			
INVENTORY											
Last Inventory Plan	3088	2240	2660	2800	2800	2450	2050	2050	1800	2150	2100
Current Inventory Plan	2240	2660	2800	2950	2950	2698	2338	2338	2093	2422	2401
Actual	2240	2660	2800	2950	2950						
Difference	-848	420	140	150	150						

Some companies store all the different versions of the plan in the S&OP database, while others archive the approved sales and operations plans at the end of each planning cycle. In each case, saving the prior S&OP data allows them to see how much the plan has changed over time – beginning of the year plan versus mid-year updates versus current plan for example.

Inventory and Backlog Targets
Since there are many situations where the planned inventory or backlog is different from the target or desired inventory or backlog, many companies find it helpful to track and display target inventory or backlog levels. The inventory target level may be defined month by month, or as a single number "desired number of months of inventory coverage", or sometimes as a range of values "between x and y". The same is true for the backlog target. However even in the instances where the target is expressed as a single number, it would typically be converted to a period by period target and shown with the other time phased plans in the inventory/backlog section of the S&OP report.

Figure 3 – 3 is an example of how the time phased inventory data might appear when inventory target data is added to a make-to-stock display. Specifically notice the line *Target*. In this example, the inventory target is calculated as the sum of twelve months of future sales divided by the desired number of turns.

Figure 3 – 3
Inventory Target Data

CALENDAR		History			Year-to-Date	Current		Current Year	Next Year		
	CUM	AUG	SEP	OCT	Planned	NOV	DEC	Planned	JAN	FEB	MAR
ANNUAL OPERATING PLAN					Year-to-Date YTD Results			Current Year Expected Results			
Budgeted Sales	14300	2000	2300	2100	20700	2100	2200	25000	2345	2471	3171
Perf to Budget	17440	1680	1330	1950	22400	2002	2110	26512			
Cum Diff Perf to Budget	3140	2820	1850	1700	1700	1602	1512	1512			
SALES	CUM				YTD Results			Expected Results			
Last Sales Plan	16172	1960	2268	2000	22400	2100	2200	26700	2400	2500	3200
Current Sales Plan	17440	1680	1330	1950	22400	2002	2110	26512	2345	2471	3171
Actual Sales	17440	1680	1330	1950	22400						
Difference	1268	-280	-938	-50							
Cum Difference	1268	988	50	0							
SHIPMENTS	CUM				YTD Results			Expected Results			
Customer Orders by Promised Date	17440	1680	1330	1950	22400			26512			
Actual Shipments	17440	1680	1330	1950	22400						
SUPPLY	CUM				YTD Results			Expected Results			
Last Supply Plan	12110	1960	2268	2000	18338	1750	1800	21888	2150	2850	3150
Current Supply Plan	12530	2100	1470	2100	18200	1750	1750	21700	2100	2800	3150
Actual Supply	12530	2100	1470	2100	18200						
Difference	420	140	-798	100	-138						
Cum Difference	420	560	-238	-138	-138						
INVENTORY					YTD Results			Expected Results			
Target	2342	2384	2382	2384	2384	2398	2440	2440	2463	2475	2424
Last Inventory Plan	3088	2240	2660	2800	2800	2450	2050	2050	1800	2150	2100
Current Inventory Plan	2240	2660	2800	2950	2950	2698	2338	2338	2093	2422	2401
Actual	2240	2660	2800	2950	2950						
Difference	-848	420	140	150	150						

Figure 3 – 4 is an example of how the time phased backlog data might appear when backlog target data is added. In this example, the backlog target (*Target Projection*) for a period is calculated as the average week's shipment (the sum of three months of future shipments divided by 13) multiplied by the desired number of weeks of backlog. Because this is a make-to-order family, shipments equal the supply plan.

Figure 3 – 4
Backlog Target Data

CALENDAR		History			Year-to-Date	Current		Current Year	Next Year		
	CUM	AUG	SEP	OCT	Planned	NOV	DEC	Expected Results	JAN	FEB	MAR
ANNUAL OPERATING PLAN	CUM				Year-to-Date YTD Results			Expected Results			
Budgeted Sales	14300	1500	1795	2000	19595	1820	1400	22815	1400	1400	1540
Perf to Budget	14385	1400	1645	1750	19180	1820	1400	22400			
Cum Diff Perf to Budget	85	-15	-165	-415	-415	-415	-415	-415			
SALES	CUM				YTD Results			Expected Results			
Last Sales Plan	14000	1470	1890	1820	19180	1820	1400	22400	1400	1400	1540
Current Sales Plan	14385	1400	1645	1750	19180	1820	1400	22400	1400	1400	1540
Actual Sales	14385	1400	1645	1750	19180						
Difference	395	-70	-245	-70	0						
Cum Difference	385	315	70	0	0						
SHIPMENTS	CUM				YTD Results			Expected Results			
Customer Orders by Promised Date	14000	1470	1890	1820	19180	1820	1470	22470	1540	280	0
Actual Shipments	14014	1456	1890	1820	19180						
SUPPLY	CUM				YTD Results			Expected Results			
Last Supply Plan	14000	1470	1890	1820	19180	1820	1470	22470	1540	1540	1540
Current Supply Plan	14014	1456	1890	1820	19180	1820	1470	22470	1540	1540	1540
Actual Supply	14014	1456	1890	1820	19180						
Difference	14	-14	0	0	0						
Cum Difference	14	0	0	0	0						
BACKLOG					YTD Results			Expected Results			
Target Projection	4782	5105	4717	4458	4458	4200	4265	4265	4265	4265	4394
Last Backlog Plan	5110	5481	5425	5180	5180	5180	5110	5110	4970	4830	4830
Current Backlog Plan	5481	5425	5180	5110	5110	5110	5040	5040	4900	4760	4760
Actual	5481	5425	5180	5110	5110						
Difference	371	-56	-245	-70	-70						

Inventory Turnover and Backlog Weeks

One common way of expressing inventory performance is as "inventory turnover" or as inventory coverage. Inventory turnover is an expression of the number of times that the inventory will be shipped and replaced (cycled or "turned over") during the course of the year. Inventory coverage represents the amount of time required to complete one inventory cycle or turn. Inventory coverage is typically expressed as days, weeks or months of coverage.

A common way to express backlog performance is as "days, weeks or months of backlog". In this calculation, the number of days, weeks or months of backlog represents the amount of time required to ship the current backlog of customer orders, at the current shipping rate.

Chapter 3 Additional Reporting Considerations 39

Figure 3 – 5 is an example of how the time phased inventory data might appear when inventory turnover data is added to a make-to-stock display.

In this example, the *Projected Turn* for any given month is calculated as the sum of the next twelve months sales (actual sales in the past periods, sales plan in the future) divided by the month end inventory. (Note that this is not the only way to calculate inventory turns, but it is typical. The inventory exists and will "turn over" based on anticipated future demand, not based on historical usage, and consequently this calculation is the most reflective of future inventory performance.) The *Number of Days* of inventory for any month is equal to 365 (days in a year) divided by the projected turn for that same month.

Figure 3 – 5
Projected Turns and Days Coverage

CALENDAR	CUM	History AUG	SEP	OCT	Year-to-Date Planned	Current NOV	DEC	Current Year Planned	Next Year JAN	FEB	MAR
ANNUAL OPERATING PLAN					Year-to-Date YTD Results			Current Year Expected Results			
Budgeted Sales	14300	2000	2300	2100	20700	2100	2200	25000	2345	2471	3171
Perf to Budget	17440	1680	1330	1950	22400	2002	2110	26512			
Cum Diff Perf to Budget	3140	2820	1850	1700	1700	1602	1512	1512			
SALES	CUM				YTD Results			Expected Results			
Last Sales Plan	16172	1960	2268	2000	22400	2100	2200	26700	2400	2500	3200
Current Sales Plan	17440	1680	1330	1950	22400	2002	2110	26512	2345	2471	3171
Actual Sales	17440	1680	1330	1950	22400						
Difference	1268	-280	-938	-50							
Cum Difference	1268	988	50	0							
SHIPMENTS	CUM				YTD Results			Expected Results			
Customer Orders by Promised Date	17440	1680	1330	1950	22400			26512			
Actual Shipments	17440	1680	1330	1950	22400						
SUPPLY	CUM				YTD Results			Expected Results			
Last Supply Plan	12110	1960	2268	2000	18338	1750	1800	21888	2150	2850	3150
Current Supply Plan	12530	2100	1470	2100	18200	1750	1750	21700	2100	2800	3150
Actual Supply	12530	2100	1470	2100	18200						
Difference	420	140	-798	100	-138						
Cum Difference	420	560	-238	-138	-138						
INVENTORY					YTD Results			Expected Results			
Target	2342	2384	2382	2384	2384	2398	2440	2440	2463	2475	2424
Last Inventory Plan	3088	2240	2660	2800	2800	2450	2050	2050	1800	2150	2100
Current Inventory Plan	2240	2660	2800	2950	2950	2698	2338	2338	2093	2422	2401
Actual	2240	2660	2800	2950	2950						
Difference	-848	420	140	150	150						
Projected Turns		10.4	10.2	9.7	9.7	11.7	14.3	14.3	14.2	13.8	13.9
Number of Days		35.1	35.8	37.6	37.6	31.1	25.6	25.6	25.6	26.4	26.3

40 SALES AND OPERATIONS PLANNING STANDARD SYSTEM

Figure 3 – 6 is an example of how the time phased backlog data might appear when weeks of backlog data is added. In this example, the *Backlog in Weeks* is calculated from the month end backlog divided by the average weekly production over the next three months (actual production in past months, production plan in the future). Average weekly production is calculated from the sum of three months' demand divided by 13 (the average number of weeks in a three month period).

Again note that just like in the case of the inventory turnover and inventory days on hand calculation, this is not the only way of calculating the size of the backlog in days or weeks. It is fairly typical though – the amount of time covered by the backlog reflects the planned shipping rate in the future not what was shipped in the past.

Figure 3-6
Backlog in Weeks

CALENDAR	CUM	History			Year-to-Date	Current		Current Year	Next Year		
		AUG	SEP	OCT	Planned	NOV	DEC		JAN	FEB	MAR
ANNUAL OPERATING PLAN	CUM				Year-to-Date YTD Results			Expected Results			
Budgeted Sales	14300	1500	1795	2000	19595	1820	1400	22815	1400	1400	1540
Perf to Budget	14385	1400	1645	1750	19180	1820	1400	22400			
Cum Diff Perf to Budget	85	-15	-165	-415	-415	-415	-415	-415			
SALES	CUM				YTD Results			Expected Results			
Last Sales Plan	14000	1470	1890	1820	19180	1820	1400	22400	1400	1400	1540
Current Sales Plan	14385	1400	1645	1750	19180	1820	1400	22400	1400	1400	1540
Actual Sales	14385	1400	1645	1750	19180						
Difference	385	-70	-245	-70	0						
Cum Difference	385	315	70	0	0						
SHIPMENTS	CUM				YTD Results			Expected Results			
Customer Orders by Promised Date	14000	1470	1890	1820	19180	1820	1470	22470	1540	280	0
Actual Shipments	14014	1456	1890	1820	19180						
SUPPLY	CUM				YTD Results			Expected Results			
Last Supply Plan	14000	1470	1890	1820	19180	1820	1470	22470	1540	1540	1540
Current Supply Plan	14014	1456	1890	1820	19180	1820	1470	22470	1540	1540	1540
Actual Supply	14014	1456	1890	1820	19180						
Difference	14	-14	0	0	0						
Cum Difference	14	0	0	0	0						
BACKLOG					YTD Results			Expected Results			
Last Backlog Plan	5110	5481	5425	5180	5180	5180	5110	5110	4970	4830	4830
Current Backlog Plan	5481	5425	5180	5110	5110	5110	5040	5040	4900	4760	4760
Actual	5481	5425	5180	5110	5110						
Difference	371	-56	-245	-70	-70						
Backlog in Weeks		12.8	13.2	13.8	13.8	14.8	14.4	14.4	14.0	13.6	13.2

Commentary

Commentary on factors that may affect the sales and operations plan are typically shown below the "hard numbers" that are shown in the time phased plan. Commentary on the hard numbers themselves – "what caused past performance to occur as it did?", "what assumptions are in the sales plan?", "what assumptions are in the supply plan?", "what is the status of key new products being introduced to the marketplace?" – as well as management decisions and more subjective data can be recorded here and made part of the official record of the sales and operations planning process. This typically takes the form of free form text shown immediately below the time phased data, or sometimes on a separate worksheet.

Putting All the Basics Together

Refer to Chapter 10 for information about accessing the S&OP displays showing the key elements discussed in chapters 2 and 3. Refer to Chapter 8 for a discussion of converting the quantitative S&OP data to graphs, particularly in support of the executive S&OP meeting.

Chapter 4
Additional Issues – Managing Change, Validation, and Linking

Managing Change

As should be clear from the discussion up to this point, an essential part of an effective S&OP process is managing the rate of change to the supply plan over time. It really isn't a question of *whether* an S&OP supply plan will ever change, it's a question of *how fast can the change be made* or *when can the change be implemented*. Customers change their minds every day and the cumulative effect in the market may represent a significant change in demand. The forecast of demand is notoriously inaccurate, and even the most sensible strategies for buffering demand variability with inventory will sometimes prove wrong. Even the things thought to be under the company's control – manufacturing output, for example – sometimes suffer from performance problems. And when any or all of these events happen, the plan may require adjustment.

Time Fence and Customer Delivery Time

The longer the lead time to procure and manufacture products the more difficult it will be to change the plan. Changing the plan many months into the future may have little impact on either material or capacity and minimal cost effect, while a similar change in the current month may be difficult, if not impossible, in terms of material availability and required capacity adjustments, and unreasonably expensive even when it is possible.

Knowing the "critical time fence[18]" for a family of products can be helpful in defining how much effort and how much analysis should be done before agreeing to a change in the plan. Inside the critical time fence, major factors to consider include the amount of potential disruption in the factory and at suppliers, the potential extra cost (air freight, overtime, etc.), the impact on other

---

[18] The critical time fence (CTF) is typically set from the cumulative lead time, considering purchasing and procurement, manufacturing and finishing lead times through the critical path, and any strategic stocking decisions for long lead time components. Strategic stocking programs reduce the critical time fence.

Since the critical time fence may actually be different from product to product within the family, either an average or a weighted average or management judgment must be applied to get the number for S&OP.

commitments (especially to customers), and the amount of increased inventory investment by delaying parts of the schedule that have already been partially complete.

It is also helpful to know the customer's expectation with respect to delivery lead time. Is the customer lead time shorter or longer than the critical time fence? Is it in line with the current delivery lead times as represented by the planned backlog? Knowing these answers can be particularly helpful in focusing improvement efforts (in cases where the current backlog grossly exceeds the customer lead time, and the critical time fence is relatively far in the future), or to gain competitive advantage (in cases where the current backlog is significantly shorter than the customer expectation).

For these reasons, both the delivery lead time and the critical time fence are typically among the other pieces of descriptive data on a typical S&OP report.

Validation

Another key part to the S&OP process is validation: developing demand and supply plans that are reasonable, and agreeing as an organization that everyone will work to them. This is what a company game plan really is.

Converting to Other Meaningful Measures

Because so many different parts of the organization participate in the S&OP process, there are occasions where the numbers, stated in a primary unit of measure, don't mean much to one group or another. Manufacturing may think in kilograms while sales deals with sales dollars. Finance may plan in cost dollars while engineering is interested in design hours. Agreeing to a plan without really understanding its consequences is an invitation to an S&OP process that does not work.

Sales and operations planning software must provide some method of converting sales plans and supply plans from the primary unit of measure to units of measure more meaningful to finance, manufacturing, engineering, sales and marketing, etc. The simple purpose of this type of calculation is to convey the needs in terms that are easily communicated and that best fit the specific area. This may mean displaying the sales and operations plan in the primary unit of measure and also in one or more alternate units: sales dollars for sales and marketing; cost dollars for finance; pieces, hours, or tons for manufacturing; engineering design hours for product engineering; etc. Other than converting all the numbers from the primary to the alternate unit of measure, nothing else changes in the format of the display.

High/Low Planning

Sometimes it is useful to formally discuss the range of the demand (high/low/most likely) as part of the S&OP process, as a way to understand the inventory and backlog consequences and the risks associated with a given supply plan. If the supply plan is not set properly, *high* sales performance may cause dangerously low inventories, backorders, excessive customer lead times and large backlogs. Similarly, *low* sales performance may cause excess inventory and the risk of obsolescence, tie up too much working capital, starve the plant of work, etc.

For this reason, many companies make a formal *high* and *low* estimate and use the S&OP system to evaluate the consequences. Examples of this can be seen in Figure 4 – 1 (make-to-stock), Figure 4 – 2 (make-to-order), and Figure 4 – 3 (finish-to-order).

In Figure 4 – 1, notice specifically the *High Sales Plan, Low Sales Plan, High Sales Inventory Plan,* and *Low Sales Inventory Plan* lines that have been added to the S&OP display. The *High Sales Inventory Plan* is calculated from the prior period inventory, the *High Sales Plan* and the *Current Supply Plan.* The *Low Sales Inventory Plan* is calculated from the prior period inventory, the *Low Sales Plan* and the *Current Supply Plan.*

Figure 4 – 1
High/Low Planning (make-to-stock)

CALENDAR		History			Year-to-Date	Current		Current Year	Next Year		
	CUM	AUG	SEP	OCT	Planned	NOV	DEC	Planned	JAN	FEB	MAR
ANNUAL OPERATING PLAN					Year-to-Date YTD Results			Current Year Expected Results			
Budgeted Sales	14300	2000	2300	2100	20700	2100	2200	25000	2345	2471	3171
Perf to Budget	17440	1680	1330	1950	22400	2002	2110	26512			
Cum Diff Perf to Budget	3140	2820	1850	1700	1700	1602	1512	1512			
SALES	CUM				YTD Results			Expected Results			
Last Sales Plan	16172	1960	2268	2000	22400	2100	2200	26700	2400	2500	3200
Current Sales Plan	17440	1680	1330	1950	22400	2002	2110	26512	2345	2471	3171
High Sales Plan						2320	2450	27170	2814	2965	3805
Low Sales Plan						1920	1920	26240	1876	1977	2537
Actual Sales	17440	1680	1330	1950	22400						
Difference	1268	-280	-938	-50							
Cum Difference	1268	988	50	0							
SHIPMENTS	CUM				YTD Results			Expected Results			
Customer Orders by Promised Date	17440	1680	1330	1950	22400			26512			
Actual Shipments	17440	1680	1330	1950	22400						
SUPPLY	CUM				YTD Results			Expected Results			
Last Supply Plan	12110	1960	2268	2000	18338	1750	1800	21888	2150	2850	3150
Current Supply Plan	12530	2100	1470	2100	18200	1750	1750	21700	2100	2800	3150
Actual Supply	12530	2100	1470	2100	18200						
Difference	420	140	-798	100	-138						
Cum Difference	420	560	-238	-138	-138						
INVENTORY					YTD Results			Expected Results			
Last Inventory Plan	3088	2240	2660	2800	2800	2450	2050	2050	1800	2150	2100
Current Inventory Plan	2240	2660	2800	2950	2950	2698	2338	2338	2093	2422	2401
High Sales Inventory Plan						2380	1998	1998	1284	1119	464
Low Sales Inventory Plan						2780	2528	2528	2752	3575	4188
Actual	2240	2660	2800	2950	2950						
Difference	-848	420	140	150	150						

46 SALES AND OPERATIONS PLANNING STANDARD SYSTEM

In Figure 4 – 2, notice specifically the *High Sales Plan, Low Sales Plan, High Sales Backlog Plan,* and *Low Sales Backlog Plan* lines that have been added to the S&OP display.

The *High Sales Backlog Plan* is calculated from the prior period backlog, the *High Sales Plan* and the *Current Supply Plan*. The *Low Sales Backlog Plan* is calculated from the prior period backlog, the *Low Sales Plan* and the *Current Supply Plan*.

Figure 4 – 2
High/Low Planning (make-to-order)

CALENDAR	CUM	History AUG	SEP	OCT	Year-to-Date Planned	Current NOV	DEC	Current Year	Next Year JAN	FEB	MAR
ANNUAL OPERATING PLAN	CUM				Year-to-Date YTD Results			Expected Results			
Budgeted Sales	14300	1500	1795	2000	19595	1820	1400	22815	1400	1400	1540
Perf to Budget	14385	1400	1645	1750	19180	1820	1400	22400			
Cum Diff Perf to Budget	85	-15	-165	-415	-415	-415	-415	-415			
SALES	CUM				YTD Results			Expected Results			
Last Sales Plan	14000	1470	1890	1820	19180	1820	1400	22400	1400	1400	1540
Current Sales Plan	14385	1400	1645	1750	19180	1820	1400	22400	1400	1400	1540
High Sales Plan						1911	1470	22561	1470	1470	1617
Low Sales Plan						1729	1330	22239	1330	1330	1463
Actual Sales	14385	1400	1645	1750	19180						
Difference	385	-70	-245	-70	0						
Cum Difference	385	315	70	0	0						
SHIPMENTS	CUM				YTD Results			Expected Results			
Customer Orders by Promised Date	14000	1470	1890	1820	19180	1820	1470	22470	1540	280	0
Actual Shipments	14014	1456	1890	1820	19180						
SUPPLY	CUM				YTD Results			Expected Results			
Last Supply Plan	14000	1470	1890	1820	19180	1820	1470	22470	1540	1540	1540
Current Supply Plan	14014	1456	1890	1820	19180	1820	1470	22470	1540	1540	1540
Actual Supply	14014	1456	1890	1820	19180						
Difference	14	-14	0	0	0						
Cum Difference	14	0	0	0	0						
BACKLOG					YTD Results			Expected Results			
Last Backlog Plan	5110	5481	5425	5180	5180	5180	5110	5110	4970	4830	4830
Current Backlog Plan	5481	5425	5180	5110	5110	5110	5040	5040	4900	4760	4760
High Sales Backlog Plan						5201	5201	5201	5131	5061	5138
Low Sales Backlog Plan						5019	4970	4970	4760	4550	4473
Actual	5481	5425	5180	5110	5110						
Difference	371	-56	-245	-70	-70						

In Figure 4 – 3, notice specifically the *High Sales Plan, Low Sales Plan, High Shipments Plan, Low Shipments Plan, High Shipment Inventory Plan, Low Shipment Inventory Plan, High Sales Backlog Plan,* and *Low Sales Backlog Plan* lines that have been added to the S&OP display.

The *High Shipment Inventory Plan* is calculated from the prior period inventory, the *High Shipments Plan* and the *Current Supply Plan*. The *Low Shipment Inventory Plan* is calculated from the prior period inventory, the *Low Shipments Plan* and the *Current Supply Plan*.

The *High Sales Backlog Plan* is calculated from the prior period backlog, the *High Sales Plan* and the *High Shipments Plan*. The *Low Sales Backlog Plan* is calculated from the prior period backlog, the *Low Sales Plan* and the *Low Shipments Plan*.

Figure 4 – 3
High/Low Planning (finish-to-order)

CALENDAR	CUM	History AUG	History SEP	History OCT	Year-to-Date Planned	Current NOV	Current DEC	Current Year	Next Year JAN	Next Year FEB	Next Year MAR
					Year-to-Date			Expected Results			
ANNUAL OPERATING PLAN											
Budgeted Sales	14300	1500	1795	2000	19595	1820	1400	22815	1400	1400	1540
Perf to Budget	14385	1400	1645	1750	19180	1820	1400	22400			
Percent Perf to Budget	101%	93%	92%	88%	98%	100%	100%	98%			
Cum Diff Perf to Budget	85	-15	-165	-415	-415	-415	-415	-415			
SALES					YTD Results			Expected Results			
Last Sales Plan	14500	1470	1890	1820	19680	1820	1400	22900	1400	1400	1540
Current Sales Plan	14385	1400	1645	1750	19180	1820	1400	22400	1400	1400	1540
High Sales Plan						1911	1470	22561	1470	1470	1617
Low Sales Plan						1729	1330	22239	1330	1330	1463
Actual Sales	14385	1400	1645	1750	19180						
Difference	-115	-70	-245	-70	-500						
Cum Difference	-115	-185	-430	-500	-500						
FINISHING AND SHIPMENTS (Finished Product)					YTD Results			Expected Results			
Last Shipments Plan	14500	1470	1890	1820	19680	1820	1470	22970	1400	1400	1540
Current Shipments Plan	14000	1470	1890	1820	19180	1820	1470	22470	1400	1400	1540
High Shipments Plan						1911	1470	22561	1470	1470	1617
Low Shipments Plan						1729	1330	22239	1330	1330	1463
Customer Orders by Promised Date	15470	1470	1890	1820	19180	1820	0	22470			
Actual Shipments	14000	1470	1890	1820	19180						
					YTD Results			Expected Results			
SUPPLY (Semi-finished material)											
Last Supply Plan	14000	1470	1890	1820	19180	1820	1470	22470	1540	1540	1540
Current Supply Plan	14000	1456	1904	1820	19180	1820	1470	22470	1540	1540	1540
Actual Supply	14000	1456	1904	1820	19180						
Difference	0	-14	14	0	0						
Cum Difference	0	-14	0	0	0						
					YTD Results			Expected Results			
SEMI-FINISHED INVENTORY											
Target	1600	1623	1629	1643	1643	1649	1672	1672	1702	1731	1748
Last Inventory Plan	1250	1750	1736	1750	1750	1750	1750	1750	1890	2030	2030
Current Inventory Plan	1750	1736	1750	1750	1750	1750	1750	1750	1890	2030	2030
High Shipment Inventory Plan						1659	1750	1750	1820	1890	1813
Low Shipment Inventory Plan						1841	1890	1890	2100	2310	2387
Actual	1750	1736	1750	1750	1750						
Difference	500	-14	14	0	0						
					YTD Results			Expected Results			
BACKLOG											
Last Backlog Plan	1820	2205	2135	1890	1890	1890	1820	1820	1820	1820	1820
Current Backlog Plan	2205	2135	1890	1820	1820	1820	1750	1750	1750	1750	1750
High Sales Backlog Plan						1820	1820	1820	1820	1820	1820
Low Sales Backlog Plan						1820	1820	1820	1820	1820	1820
Actual	2205	2135	1890	1820	1820						
Difference	385	-70	-245	-70	-70						

Converting S&OP Data to Daily Rates

Both the agreed sales and supply plans are typically stated as the rate per month for the type of product or a family of products. To assist in validating these rates, it is sometimes helpful to view them in a different way – based on rates per selling or manufacturing day. For example, the sales plan from one month to the next may change from 500 to 550 – a period increase of 10% - which seems reasonable. However, if the number of sales days per period drops from 22 to 17, this sales rate can be seen to be an increase from 22.7 units per day to a rate of 32.4 per day – an increase of nearly 50% per day! Similarly, a supply plan for a period containing a two week plant shutdown looks very different when viewed as a daily rate.

Consequently converting the sales plan per month to sales per day, and the supply plan per month to supply per day can be a helpful conversion. Sales per day and supply per day can be among the simplest ways to validate future plans.

The calculations for daily sales and daily supply rates are:

Average daily sales = Sales plan / selling days in the period

Average daily supply = Supply plan / supply days in the period

Example 4 - 4 shows a sales and operations planning report with conversions to daily rates. Notice specifically the lines *Sales Days* and *Supply Days* in the Calendar section of the display, and the calculated rates shown in *Sales Plan Per Day* and *Supply Plan Per Day*.

Chapter 4 Additional Issues 49

Figure 4-4
Conversion to Daily Rates

CALENDAR	CUM	AUG	History SEP	OCT	Year-to-Date Planned	Current NOV	DEC	Current Year Planned	Next Year JAN	FEB	MAR
Sales Days	136	23	20	22	201	19	20	240	22	20	22
Supply Days	136	23	20	22	201	19	20	240	22	20	22
					Year-to-Date			Current Year			
ANNUAL OPERATING PLAN					YTD Results			Expected Results			
Budgeted Sales	14300	2000	2300	2100	20700	2100	2200	25000	2345	2471	3171
Perf to Budget	17440	1680	1330	1950	22400	2002	2110	26512			
Cum Diff Perf to Budget	3140	2820	1850	1700	1700	1602	1512	1512			
SALES	CUM				YTD Results			Expected Results			
Last Sales Plan	16172	1960	2268	2000	22400	2100	2200	26700	2400	2500	3200
Current Sales Plan	17440	1680	1330	1950	22400	2002	2110	26512	2345	2471	3171
Actual Sales	17440	1680	1330	1950	22400						
Difference	1268	-280	-938	-50							
Cum Difference	1268	988	50	0							
Sales Plan Per Day	128.2	73.0	66.5	88.6	111.4	105.4	105.5	110.5	106.6	123.6	144.1
SHIPMENTS	CUM				YTD Results			Expected Results			
Customer Orders by Promised Date	17440	1680	1330	1950	22400			26512			
Actual Shipments	17440	1680	1330	1950	22400						
SUPPLY	CUM				YTD Results			Expected Results			
Last Supply Plan	12110	1960	2268	2000	18338	1750	1800	21888	2150	2850	3150
Current Supply Plan	12530	2100	1470	2100	18200	1750	1750	21700	2100	2800	3150
Actual Supply	12530	2100	1470	2100	18200						
Difference	420	140	-798	100	-138						
Cum Difference	420	560	-238	-138	-138						
Supply Plan Per Day	92.1	91.3	73.5	95.5	90.5	92.1	87.5	90.4	95.5	140.0	143.2
					YTD Results			Expected Results			
INVENTORY											
Last Inventory Plan	3088	2240	2660	2800	2800	2450	2050	2050	1800	2150	2100
Current Inventory Plan	2240	2660	2800	2950	2950	2698	2338	2338	2093	2422	2401
Actual	2240	2660	2800	2950	2950						
Difference	-848	420	140	150	150						

Converting S&OP Data to Takt Time

Similarly, in lean manufacturing environments, one of the best methods for validating the sales and operations plan is the takt time calculation. Takt time and operational takt time are expressions of sales and production rates. Takt time indicates what the marketplace would like for output – one unit every X seconds or minutes. Operational takt time reflects any decisions made about inventory levels or other factors related to the way management wants to operate – one unit every Y seconds or minutes because of an inventory build or temporary overtime, for example.

Most importantly for the purposes of S&OP, these numbers for future time periods show the relationship between what the market wants (takt), how the plant would like to operate (operational takt), and the capability of the plant as designed. Mismatches between the capability of the plant – the engineered cycle time – and the operational takt time should be visible in S&OP with sufficient lead time to ensure that capabilities can be made to match demand.

The calculations for takt and operational takt time are:

> Takt time = Effective working time in the period / Sales plan for the period
>
> Operational takt time = Adjusted working time in the period / Supply plan for the period

To calculate takt time for any given period, the software must have access to the calendar data for working time in that period. To properly calculate operational takt time, the software must be capable of recognizing temporary adjustments to the calendar as well as any inventory adjustments (which are reflected in a supply plan different from the sales plan).

Figure 4 – 5 shows a sales and operations plan and the calculated takt and operational takt times for each period. Two lines of data, *Normal Production Hours* and *Adjustment (Hours)*, have been added to the Calendar section, the calculated takt time is shown in the *Takt Time* line, and the calculated operational takt time and a comparison to the designed cycle time for the finishing process are shown in the lines *Operational Takt Time* and *Cell Design Cycle Time*.

In this example, the designed cycle time (Design C/T) is set between 225 and 350 seconds – in other words the finishing process or finishing cell is designed to be operated within this range – and operational takt times outside the range will be flagged by a message (ERROR) in the *Cell Design Cycle Time* line. Operational takt times supported by the designed cycle time are noted "OK".

Chapter 4 Additional Issues 51

Figure 4 - 5
S&OP with Takt Times

CALENDAR			History		Year-to-Date	Current		Current Year	Next Year		
	CUM	AUG	SEP	OCT	Planned	NOV	DEC	Planned	JAN	FEB	MAR
Supply Days	136	23	20	22	201	19	20	240	22	20	22
Normal Production Hours	1088	184	160	176	1608	152	160	1920	176	160	176
Adjustment (Hours)	0	0	0	0	0	0	0	0	0	22	22
					Year-to-Date			Current Year			
ANNUAL OPERATING PLAN					YTD Results			Expected Results			
Budgeted Sales	14300	2000	2300	2100	20700	2100	2200	25000	2345	2471	3171
Perf to Budget	17440	1680	1330	1950	22400	2002	2110	26512			
Cum Diff Perf to Budget	3140	2820	1850	1700	1700	1602	1512	1512			
SALES	CUM				YTD Results			Expected Results			
Last Sales Plan	16172	1960	2268	2000	22400	2100	2200	26700	2400	2500	3200
Current Sales Plan	17440	1680	1330	1950	22400	2002	2110	26512	2345	2471	3171
Actual Sales	17440	1680	1330	1950	22400						
Difference	1268	-280	-938	-50							
Cum Difference	1268	988	50	0							
Takt Time (seconds)		338.0	254.0	316.8		273.3	273.0	260.7	270.2	233.1	199.8
SHIPMENTS	CUM				YTD Results			Expected Results			
Customer Orders by Promised Date	17440	1680	1330	1950	22400			26512			
Actual Shipments	17440	1680	1330	1950	22400						
SUPPLY	CUM				YTD Results			Expected Results			
Last Supply Plan	12110	1960	2268	2000	18338	1750	1800	21888	2150	2850	3150
Current Supply Plan	12530	2100	1470	2100	18200	1750	1750	21700	2100	2800	3150
Actual Supply	12530	2100	1470	2100	18200						
Difference	420	140	-798	100	-138						
Cum Difference	420	560	-238	-138	-138						
Operational Takt Time (sec)		315.4	391.8	301.7	318.1	312.7	329.1	318.5	301.7	234.0	226.3
Cell Design Cycle Time		OK	ERROR	OK		OK	OK	OK	OK	OK	OK
INVENTORY					YTD Results			Expected Results			
Last Inventory Plan	3088	2240	2660	2800	2800	2450	2050	2050	1800	2150	2100
Current Inventory Plan	2240	2660	2800	2950	2950	2698	2338	2338	2093	2422	2401
Actual	2240	2660	2800	2950	2950						
Difference	-848	420	140	150	150						

Rough-cut Planning
Perhaps the most important method for validating the sales and operations plan is "rough-cut planning". In fact this method is so important that we'll cover it in a separate chapter, all its own.

Linkages
The sales plan and supply plan from the S&OP process are the primary drivers for all other detailed plans (master production schedule, material plan, capacity plan, supplier schedule, etc.) in a formal resource planning system. These plans also drive lean planning processes which depend on takt time and operational takt time.

Because senior management participates in the process of developing and approving the sales and operations plan – and won't typically get involved in detailed planning and scheduling activities on a day to day basis – it is essential that a mechanism exists to keep the detailed plans synchronized with the high level plans. If they diverge over time, then results will be very different from what was expected. And the more that real performance differs from anticipated performance, the more likely the S&OP process will suffer and degrade.

The two primary linkages that must be maintained are the link between the S&OP sales plan and the detailed forecasts, and the link between the S&OP supply plan and the master production schedule.

Linking the S&OP Sales Plan to Detailed Forecasts
The sales plan used for S&OP for the product family must agree with the sum of the individual demands (typically forecasts) for items within the family. In some cases, the sales plan for the family will be developed from the sum of the forecasts, customer orders, and distribution demands for individual items within the family. In other cases, the sales plan for the family might be prorated into detailed sales forecasts for individual items within the family. For example, if the sales plan for the family is 1000, and one item is 10% of the family, the forecast for the item will be 100.

A complicating factor for many companies is the fact that the horizon for detailed sales planning is shorter than the horizon for S&OP. In some companies this may be because of the number of new products. In situations where a high percentage of future sales will be coming from products that aren't yet designed, it may make sense to forecast in detail only a few months into the future and forecast total volume, irrespective of the individual SKUs, at the S&OP family level for the subsequent periods. Or it may make sense to forecast existing products over a long horizon, and at the S&OP family level forecast the additional new product volume, again irrespective of SKU detail.

Other companies may choose to cut off their detailed sales planning horizons because of the amount of variability in the demand. It may not make sense, after some point in time, to even consider the sum of the detailed forecasts for planning activities. As long as the cut-off date is after the critical time fence, and there are no complicating seasonality issues, it makes sense to forecast detail over a shorter horizon than the volume forecasts used in S&OP.

Forecasting less detail rather than more is the best approach for many companies. Cutting off the detailed mix forecast at the critical time fence plus some small window for visibility typically provides enough demand detail for detailed material planning, procurement, and scheduling. For periods after the time fence plus visibility, the total family forecast – the volume forecast – can be used to drive the S&OP process. In the end, enough demand data exists to drive the mix related processes like master production scheduling as well as to drive the volume related processes like S&OP and rough-cut. And no one has spent hours of unproductive time fine-tuning (or being tempted to fine-tune) mix forecasts far into the future.

Regardless of how the demand numbers for S&OP are developed or the horizon used, the S&OP sales plan and the sum of the individual detailed demands must be in agreement for the periods where they both exist. For example, if there are five items in the family and the sum of their individual forecasts in a period equal 1,100, and the sales plan for the family in that period equals 1000, then one or the other must be revised until they are equal.

Linking Supply Plans to the Master Production Schedule

Master production schedules for individual items within the family will be developed from the supply plan. The broad statement of supply must be broken down into a schedule for specific items, dates, and quantities. Working within the constraints of the supply plan, the master scheduler will develop the statement of planned future production for individual items and set the timing and quantities of individual production lots.

The supply plan and the sum of the master schedules must be in agreement if the supply plan is to truly act as a regulator of the master production schedule. If the detailed master schedules when summarized are not within a realistic tolerance of the supply plan, then the material and capacity plans will be misstated, and anticipated results as defined by the business and financial plans and by the sales and marketing plans will not be met.

The master schedules for specific items within the product family, when totaled, must equal the supply plan for the family. A good rule of thumb is that if the master production schedule differs from the supply plan by more than 5% in a period, then one or the other must be revised until they are equal (within the 5% tolerance). In addition, the cumulative difference between the supply plan and the MPS over time should approach zero.

Figure 4 - 6 shows an example of an S&OP report showing the comparison of the supply plan and the sum of the MPS. Note the new line in the SUPPLY section of the display: *Actual Supply/MPS*. This line displays the actual supply in the past, and the sum of the MPS in the future. The calculations for the *Difference* line have been modified appropriately.

Figure 4 – 6
Supply Plan to Summarized MPS Comparison

CALENDAR	CUM	AUG	History SEP	OCT	Year-to-Date Planned	Current NOV	DEC	Current Year Planned	Next Year JAN	FEB	MAR
ANNUAL OPERATING PLAN					Year-to-Date YTD Results			Current Year Expected Results			
Budgeted Sales	14300	2000	2300	2100	20700	2100	2200	25000	2345	2471	3171
Perf to Budget	17440	1680	1330	1950	22400	2002	2110	26512			
Cum Diff Perf to Budget	3140	2820	1850	1700	1700	1602	1512	1512			
SALES	CUM				YTD Results			Expected Results			
Last Sales Plan	16172	1960	2268	2000	22400	2100	2200	26700	2400	2500	3200
Current Sales Plan	17440	1680	1330	1950	22400	2002	2110	26512	2345	2471	3171
Actual Sales	17440	1680	1330	1950	22400						
Difference	1268	-280	-938	-50							
Cum Difference	1268	988	50	0							
SHIPMENTS	CUM				YTD Results			Expected Results			
Customer Orders by Promised Date	17440	1680	1330	1950	22400			26512			
Actual Shipments	17440	1680	1330	1950	22400						
SUPPLY	CUM				YTD Results			Expected Results			
Last Supply Plan	12110	1960	2268	2000	18338	1750	1800	21888	2150	2850	3150
Current Supply Plan	12530	2100	1470	2100	18200	1750	1750	21700	2100	2800	3150
Actual Supply and MPS	12530	2100	1470	2100	18200	1775	1725		2150	2850	3150
Difference	420	140	-798	100	-138	25	-25		50	50	0
Cum Difference	420	560	-238	-138	-138						
INVENTORY					YTD Results			Expected Results			
Last Inventory Plan	3088	2240	2660	2800	2800	2450	2050	2050	1800	2150	2100
Current Inventory Plan	2240	2660	2800	2950	2950	2698	2338	2338	2093	2422	2401
Actual	2240	2660	2800	2950	2950						
Difference	-848	420	140	150	150						

PART 3:
RELATED SYSTEMS

Chapter 5
Rough-Cut Planning

Perspective

The intent of rough-cut planning is to convert high-level plans into the impact on resources needed to carry out those plans. There are multiple reasons for doing rough-cut planning as part of the S&OP process:

- To provide "distance-vision" for both material and capacity needs, so the long-term plan can be validated. Having some form of visibility into future needs is particularly important for shared (non-aligned) resources. Shared resources are those that are not unique or aligned to an individual product family or value-stream[19], where the sales and operations plan for several different families determine the total capacity required.

  In a **fully** lean manufacturing environment – few of which really exist – all resources would be aligned to the individual families (value-streams) and there would be no need for rough-cut capacity planning at all. Simply looking at the supply plan opposite the demonstrated performance from the past would be enough to gauge how reasonable future supply plans are. Unfortunately even many of the best lean companies have some shared resources – often far up the value-stream – but still important enough that some long-range planning is required.

- To help in managing changes to the S&OP in response to changing market and manufacturing conditions, and in light of actual performance that may differ from the plan.

- To connect the way a company wants to operate – in its markets and in manufacturing – with its capital planning processes, particularly in those situations where long term capacity appears insufficient to meet the plan, but where the horizon for acquiring additional capacity is adequate.

Rough-cut planning converts the sales and operations plan into approximate material and capacity requirements twelve to eighteen months into the future. In

---

[19] Value-stream: a lean manufacturing term meaning all of the activities, both value-adding and non-value-adding, needed to bring a product from concept to launch, and from order to delivery.

most companies, the horizon for S&OP is significantly longer than that being used for master scheduling and material requirements planning, and as such is almost ideally suited for all these objectives.

Understanding the capacity and material implications of S&OP is the first objective of rough-cut planning. "Is there enough capacity?" – "can the key materials be made available in sufficient volumes?" – "is the desirable plan a "do-able" plan?" - these are questions that must be answered before committing to the sales and operations plan. If capacity is insufficient and more equipment or people are not available, or if material will not be available, then *do-ability* has to win out over *desirability*. It isn't enough to want something – you must have a chance of actually doing it. Otherwise, the sales and operations plan will direct purchases of material, commitment of labor and machine hours, authorize inventory levels that will not be achievable.

In most situations where plans are approved without regard to validity, the formal planning system will degenerate into a series of informal disconnected processes. One part of the organization may do things that protect its own interests, perhaps at the expense of other parts of the company and degraded business plan performance. The only way to have a "company game plan" that everyone operates to is to have a valid game plan from the start.

Managing change to the S&OP is the second objective of rough-cut. Effectively managing change may be one of the most challenging tasks in industrial management. The plan may need to change, but the dynamics of the decision include a mix of qualitative and quantitative factors. Customers and customer service are involved, often injecting more than the normal amount of emotion into the discussion. What people want to do and what the plant is capable of doing – how flexible it can be in the short term, how fast it can ramp up or down to the new supply levels, whether it can achieve the output volumes required of it – are often different things.

In these situations, there are plenty of opinions. What are really needed are facts. Problems and their effects must be reduced to alternatives with proposals for action. Managing the sales and operations plan without the means to evaluate the effects of changes on both material and capacity fails to provide a valid assessment of the alternatives. An incorrect or incomplete assessment of the alternatives may mean the wrong decision – ramping up too soon, or not soon enough, adjusting labor too quickly or not fast enough, reducing inventory to dangerously low levels and jeopardizing customer service, increasing inventory to the point where working capital levels threaten cash flow, extending customer lead times by increasing the order backlog, etc.

The only really effective way to handle changes in the sales and operations is to begin by correctly assessing the alternatives and identifying any **limitations** that must be resolved. Everyone involved must then press for a decision on any commitments that are necessary in order to resolve the limitations that exist.

Finally, rough-cut planning is the key function for driving long-term capital planning – the third objective. Here the basic idea is to predict when additional capacity will be required in advance of that need becoming a crisis, and then use the basic numbers and the process that predicted that need to justify capital expenditures. Capital planning is something every company does: S&OP and rough-cut ensure that the way the company wants to operate (the sales and operations plan) and the capital plan that guarantees that it is possible are consistent with each other.

There are two major types of rough-cut planning:

- Rough-cut capacity planning (RCCP)
- Rough-cut material planning (RCMP)

Rough-cut capacity planning is an approximate type of capacity planning using some load profiles (sometimes called "representative routings") defined for the product families, focused on key or critical work centers, lines, departments, cells, suppliers, and support areas (engineering, distribution, shipping). For rough-cut capacity planning, "key" or "critical" resources are ones that are important, although not necessarily constant bottlenecks.

Typical resources that might be planned as part of rough-cut capacity planning might include:

- Overall plant capacity
- Labor hours in total or for people with unique skills
- Assembly hours in a specific cell or bottleneck process
- Machine capacity in a key piece of equipment or unique or proprietary plant process
- Testing cell capacity
- Engineering hours needed to configure the final product to the customer's specification
- Space required in a warehouse or storage area.
- Waste or effluent release, etc.
- Shipping labor

- Design time or credit release time
- Inspection or QC time
- Supplier capacity

Rough-cut material planning is an approximate type of material planning using a simplified bill of material, often called a bill of resources. It can be used to project material requirements to key suppliers so as to bypass the need for detailed material planning way out into the future, to provide a simple, early estimate of changes in material requirements, and in some cases to bypass the need for detailed material planning entirely.

Normally, companies validate the sales and operations plan against all major resources, regardless of whether the resources are capacity or material. In most cases, the rough-cut plan will be based on the supply plan although there are instances where the limiting resource is driven by the sales, shipping, or inventory plan. For example, shipping labor is driven by the shipments plan not the supply plan. Similarly, space required in the cold storage warehouse is driven by the inventory plan not the volume of supply.

In some instances, rough-cut planning can't be done solely by product family, and has to be run using the items in the master production schedule. This can happen when resource requirements vary significantly based on the mix of items in the master schedule. In the long-term, the rough-cut planning process can plan based on average mix assumptions. In the shorter term, where the real mix is better known, the master schedule may be a better source for rough projections of capacity and material requirements.

When rough-cut planning is run directly from the master production schedule; it can be an invaluable tool for assessing changes to shorter term plans when the product mix is changing – something that S&OP cannot do.

Rough-Cut Capacity Planning

The load profiles used in rough-cut capacity planning are a way to relate product families or individual master schedule items to the key resources required to produce them. The load profiles should contain the resource identifier, an indicator of which plan (supply, sales, inventory, etc,) drives the capacity projection, number of hours, pounds, molds, etc., and the approximate offset in time from the completion date of the plan. Typically this data is set based on historical records, but where this information is not available it may be set from estimates by knowledgeable people.

It is helpful to have software that can analyze the detailed routings and help in setting and maintaining load profiles for rough-cut. To properly reflect the future capacity requirements, the load profile quantity (number of hours, pounds, molds, etc.) should somehow reflect the mix of items that will be produced. One way to do this is to "weight" the routing run times for each item based on the proportion that item represents of total production. In other words, a product that represents 50% of the total production in the family would make a larger contribution to the load profile quantity than any of the other twenty items making up the balance.

The plan is multiplied by the quantities in the load profiles and offset from the completion date to generate rough-cut capacity requirements by date. These rough-cut capacity requirements are summarized into monthly periods and displayed as a rough-cut capacity picture.

Rough-cut capacity planning has several limitations. It does not calculate detailed capacity requirements by work center, take completed parts and assemblies into account, consider work in process or partial completions, and it assumes lot-for-lot ordering in the calculation of resource requirements. In spite of these clear limitations, rough-cut capacity planning does provide a way to assess the capacity requirements created by a sales and operations plan in a rough-cut way. A plan that is grossly overstated or a change to the plan that generates a significant overload on a resource or key piece of equipment will typically be clear from a rough-cut capacity planning run.

The rough-cut capacity planning report should be similar to a typical or traditional detailed capacity requirements planning report, showing the resource number and description; actual demonstrated capacity; period date; total capacity required in the period; and total capacity available (sometimes called "planned demonstrated capacity"). Effective capacity planning must start with knowing actual demonstrated capacity. Actual demonstrated capacity – what was really done in the past – must be the starting point for any future capacity planning and the basis for making adjustments to the capacity plan going forward. Otherwise it is too easy to overstate or understate planned demonstrated capacity – in which case the capacity plan becomes a wish list of "what we'd like to do" as opposed to "what we realistically can do".

Since capacity is not a fixed single number – it can be flexed up or down based on manning, overtime, etc. – it is helpful to show both planned and maximum capacity for each period and to allow it to vary by period. (Note that "maximum capacity" in this context is what the supply chain can be reasonably expected to flex up to, not the theoretical maximum of what the machine is rated to do and perfect productivity, no scrap or rework, etc.)

To display variable capacity and variable maximum capacity by time period, the rough-cut planning software must include functions for maintaining and overriding future planned capacity numbers – starting with actual demonstrated capacity and then applying future planned changes in productivity; added people and equipment; changes in shift patterns, hours per shift, planned downtime, etc.

It is also helpful to see the required capacity for each period as well as a rolling 3 month average capacity requirement. The rolling 3 month average capacity requirement tends to help focus on the grossly overloaded situations, not the period-to-period noise built into the calculation.

A sample rough-cut capacity planning report is shown in Figure 5 – 1.

Figure 5 – 1 Rough-cut Capacity Plan

	Jan-06	Feb-06	Mar-06	Apr-06	May-06	Jun-06
CAPACITY REQUIRED						
Capacity Required	529	486	560	502	494	364
3 Month Average	525	516	519	453	517	489
PLANNED CAPACITY						
Planned Demonstrated	450	450	500	520	520	520
Reqd To Demonstrated	118%	108%	112%	97%	95%	70%
3 Month Ave To Demo	117%	115%	104%	87%	99%	94%
MAXIMUM CAPACITY						
Maximum	480	480	520	550	550	550
Reqd To Demonstrated	110%	101%	108%	91%	90%	66%
3 Month Ave To Demo	109%	108%	100%	82%	94%	89%
CUM ANALYSIS						
Cum Capacity Required	529	1015	1575	2077	2571	2935
Cum Planned Demo	450	900	1400	1920	2440	2960
Reqd to Demonstrated	118%	113%	113%	108%	105%	99%

To effectively solve rough-cut capacity planning problems, especially where a resource is shared by multiple product families, a way needs to be provided to identify the source of the capacity requirements. The simplest way is to provide a report or display that shows the individual product families causing the rough-cut capacity requirements in each time period. The detail to the rough-cut capacity report is similar to the capacity pegging report shown in Figure 5 – 2.

Figure 5 – 2
Rough-cut Capacity Pegging

	Family	Capacity Required	S&OP Period	S&OP Quantity
Jan-06	TOTAL	529		
	01 Widget	100	Jan-06	12500
	02 Pumps	120	Jan-06	18000
	03 ICE	25	Jan-06	2000
	04 Bands	4	Jan-06	500
	05 Orca	160	Jan-06	17760
	06 SLAM	120	Jan-06	15000
Feb-06	TOTAL	486		
	01 Widget	92	Feb-06	11484
	02 Pumps	110	Feb-06	16537
	03 ICE	23	Feb-06	1837
	04 Bands	4	Feb-06	459
	05 Orca	147	Feb-06	16316
	06 SLAM	110	Feb-06	13781
Mar-06	TOTAL	560		
	01 Widget	106	Mar-06	13233
	02 Pumps	127	Mar-06	19055
	03 ICE	26	Mar-06	2117
	04 Bands	4	Mar-06	529
	05 Orca	169	Mar-06	18801
	06 SLAM	127	Mar-06	15879
Apr-06	TOTAL	502		
	01 Widget	95	Apr-06	11862
	02 Pumps	114	Apr-06	17081
	03 ICE	24	Apr-06	1898
	04 Bands	4	Apr-06	474
	05 Orca	152	Apr-06	16854
	06 SLAM	114	Apr-06	14234
May-06	TOTAL	494		
	01 Widget	93	May-06	11673
	02 Pumps	112	May-06	16809
	03 ICE	23	May-06	1868
	04 Bands	4	May-06	467
	05 Orca	149	May-06	16585
	06 SLAM	112	May-06	14008

Rough-Cut Material Planning

The bill of resources used in rough-cut material planning is a way to relate product families to the key raw material and components required to produce them. Like the load profiles used for rough-cut capacity planning, the bill of resources should contain an identifier for the key component or raw material, an indicator for which plan drives the projection, the quantity per, and the approximate offset in time from the completion date of the plan.

The plan is exploded through the bill of resources and multiplied by the quantity per to generate rough-cut material requirements by date. These requirements are summarized into monthly periods and displayed as the rough-cut material plan.

Rough-cut material planning has similar limitations to rough-cut capacity planning: it fails to take completed parts and assemblies into account, disregards work in process and partial completions, and it assumes lot-for-lot ordering in the calculation of the requirements.

It would be possible to show the rough-cut material plan in a format similar to the rough-cut capacity plan (see Figure 5 – 1). However, more typically, because rough-cut material planning is a type of material planning, the report should be similar in format to traditional material planning or supplier scheduling displays and projections.

Chapter 6
Feeding Financial Analysis

Perspective

Truly effective financial planning and decision making can only be done when based on operational system drivers and data. Actual sales and supply performance, projected sales and supply plans, and inventory values from the operational planning and execution systems should drive future financial plans (cash flow, profitability, projected inventory valuation, budgeting, etc.), because the numbers in these systems are driving actions, activities, and all the detailed decisions in the areas of sales, supply, sourcing, inventory, capacity, etc.

Financial projections can be made directly from S&OP data[20] and these can feed key financial planning and analysis processes, or S&OP data can be extracted and fed to financial planning systems where projections are made. Projections based on S&OP data, and the related financial processes are the ones discussed in this chapter. More detailed financial projections can be made using the numbers in the master scheduling, material planning and capacity planning systems, but these projections are outside the scope of this book.

Financial planning and analysis activities fed by S&OP data typically include:

---

[20] The advantage of projections developed from the sales and operations plan is that they don't depend on detailed planning numbers, which may or may not exist in periods beyond a few months into the future. Of course, the principal disadvantage is that when volume numbers like the ones from the S&OP sales plan are used, assumptions have to be made about the mix of items within that volume, and additional work is required to establish average cost and selling price data based on this forecasted mix.

Since the financial projections were developed from the sales and operations plan, it is possible to look into the system and track a financial number back to sales and supply decisions causing it. A top manager or financial planner can take a number like the projected value of finished goods inventory in month three, trace it back to the projected finished goods inventory in month three for each product family, and trace this back to the sales plan and supply plan that caused it. If there is a problem with the financial plan, it is possible to see it in advance and attempt to correct it before it happens.

Notice that what we are talking about here is using S&OP to feed financial projections in the future. It is not designed to be a perfect revenue predictor for the current month. For this kind of prediction, look to the systems that manage mix not volume.

- Budgeting and business planning for future years.
- Projecting current year revenue, margin, and profit based on current sales plans and forecasts, and actual performance to date during the year.
- Reconciling revenue plans, targets and budgets from the business plan to current operational projections.
- Projecting future cash flows.
- Projecting inventory investment based upon future sales and supply levels, and planned or actual average cost of goods sold.
- Capital planning.

Budgeting and Business Planning

The dollarized sales and operations plan should be fed to the annual budgeting process. Each year, beginning several months in advance of the fiscal year, the rolling projected demand, supply, backlog, and inventory plans that exist as part of S&OP become the primary input to budgeting process. Since the sales and operations plan stretches out over an eighteen month horizon, even a company kicking off the budgeting process six months ahead of the fiscal year start date will have enough visibility into anticipated full year results. Assuming that this is the best estimate of both the marketplace and supply capabilities, in some sense it is already the "budget" for the next fiscal year. And while the numbers may change several times before the start of the next fiscal year, because their source is the S&OP process, any new data or information will immediately be reflected in the financial planning numbers used in the formal budgeting process.

There are several reasons to use the dollarized S&OP numbers in the budgeting process:

1. Product and market intelligence is already reflected in the numbers, and as conditions change, so do the sales and supply plans.
2. The numbers are easy to get and processes already exist to maintain them.
3. The numbers coming out of S&OP tend to be more valid than numbers developed outside the operational systems – they are subjected to constant scrutiny, reviewed monthly and debated across key groups and people in the organization, and they drive the detailed activities in the company. Executive

management has more confidence in these numbers because of the analysis, discussion, debate and decision-making using them each month.

The following calculations should be provided for each family of products in support of budgeting for revenue and profits[21]:

- Budgeted sales dollars: planned sales at average selling price.
- Budgeted cost dollars: planned sales at average cost of goods sold.
- Budgeted profit: budgeted sales less budgeted cost.
- Budgeted margin percentage: budgeted gross profit divided by budgeted gross sales.

Since the annual budget also covers cash flows, projections of cash receipts and cash disbursements (including material expenses, direct labor expense, and variable overhead expense) should be provided. A complete explanation of these calculations is provided later in this chapter:

Current Year Revenue and Profit Projections

The system should also provide a method for dollarizing the sales and operations plan to support current year revenue and profit planning, and comparison to the approved budget.

As part of every S&OP cycle, the current monthly sales plan (actual sales year-to-date plus planned sales in the future) should be extended by the average selling price and compared to budgeted revenue plans by month or quarter, and for the fiscal year. The current sales plan should be extended by the average cost of sales for comparison to budgeted costs, again by month or quarter, and for the fiscal year. The difference – gross profit and margin – should also be compared to budgeted profit and budgeted margin.

The cumulative financial impact of actual performance to date is particularly helpful since it is the most accurate reflection of what is happening with sales

---

[21] There are no assumptions about the specific type of cost system being used. It is possible to develop these projections using any of a number of cost systems, including standard cost, job cost, direct cost, activity-based cost, etc. The only assumption here is that some kind of cost and selling price data is available for each family of products. Since each family is a mix of many SKUs, this means that the cost and selling price figures used for the financial projections represent a weighted average of the SKU level cost and selling prices.

and costs (in light of actual unit performance and actual cost data) and, as mentioned earlier, is perhaps the best validation of the plans in place through the end of the current fiscal year.

Financial Reconciliation and Adjustment

Projected revenue, profit and cash flow plans for the current fiscal year need to be compared to the budget periodically to ensure that they remain realistic and in line with financial commitments that have been made to owners, corporate management, or senior management at the site. The natural time to do this is during the monthly S&OP process. In fact, normally financial reconciliation occurs several times during the monthly S&OP process, and the review of projected financial results is always part of the executive S&OP meeting, in companies operating successful S&OP processes.

Financial reconciliation consists of comparing the dollarized current year revenue and profit with the business plan. Knowing that the projected financial results don't match agreed budgets or targets should trigger analysis and action before anything else happens – can resources be redeployed to bring plans back in line with targets?, should marketing budgets be adjusted to focus more on families that need more promotion or additional market coverage?, would a pricing adjustment make sense to drive different volumes and perhaps different financial results?

In some cases, when there is a significant deviation, the business plan will be updated to reflect the current sales and operations plan. Generally speaking though, this will happen infrequently and for most companies no more frequently than once per year. In some cases, the sales and operations plan may be revised to reflect the business plan and to bring projected results back in line with the budgets. In the cases where neither the sales and operations plan nor the business plan are updated and are allowed to diverge, then the differences must be analyzed and communicated across the organization. The basic idea in this situation is to understand and agree to the impact of a sales and operations plan that is different from the business plan, and continue to look for ways to bring them back in line.

Figure 6 – 1 shows a typical projection of revenue and profitability as well as a comparison to the business plan. S&OP numbers have been converted to revenue and cost dollars and projected profits. The approved business plan for the same periods is shown, along with period by period variances and comparisons. Five categories of management information are displayed:

Business plan: budgeted sales at average selling price and average unit cost, budgeted profit per period, cumulative budgeted profit

Selling price and cost of sales: Average actual selling price (past periods), average planned selling price (future periods), average actual cost of goods sold (past periods) and average planned cost of goods sold (future periods).

Current sales plan: actual unit sales at actual selling price and actual cost through the current date, projected sales at average anticipated selling price and cost through the end of the year, actual and projected profit by period, cumulative profit

Profit comparison: sales plan to business plan (budget) variance by period, cumulative variance

Gross margins: budgeted versus the actual or projected by time period.

Figure 6 – 1
Revenue and Profit Projection

Family		BZK		Average Selling Price	1.960			
Description		Small Widgets		Standard Product Cost	1.140			

ALL FIGURES IN US DOLLARS

PROFITABILITY	JAN - JUL TOTAL	History AUG	SEP	OCT	Year To Date Results	Current NOV	DEC	Current Year Expected Results
Business Plan								
Budgeted Sales (Sales Dollars)	$ 2,802,800	392,000	450,800	411,600	$ 4,057,200	411,600	431,200	$ 4,900,000
Budgeted Sales (Cost Dollars)	$ 1,630,200	228,000	262,200	239,400	$ 2,359,800	239,400	250,800	$ 2,850,000
Budgeted Gross Profit	$ 1,172,600	164,000	188,600	172,200	$ 1,697,400	172,200	180,400	$ 2,050,000
Cum Budgeted Gross Profit	$ 1,172,600	1,336,600	1,525,200	1,697,400	$ 1,697,400	1,869,600	2,050,000	$ 2,050,000
ASP (Average Actual or Budget)	1.93	1.98	1.99	1.90	1.93	1.96	1.96	1.94
COGS (Average Actual or Budget)	1.14	1.14	1.14	1.14	1.14	1.14	1.14	1.14
Sales Plan								
Current Sales Plan (Actual Sales Dollars)	$ 3,365,920	332,640	264,670	370,500	$ 4,333,730	392,392	413,560	$ 5,139,682
Current Sales Plan (Cost Dollars)	$ 1,988,160	191,520	151,620	222,300	$ 2,553,600	228,228	240,540	$ 3,022,368
Current Gross Profit	$ 1,377,760	141,120	113,050	148,200	$ 1,780,130	164,164	173,020	$ 2,117,314
Current Cum Gross Profit	$ 1,377,760	1,518,880	1,631,930	1,780,130	$ 1,780,130	1,944,294	2,117,314	$ 2,117,314
Sales Plan to Business Plan Profit Comparison								
Current Sales Plan vs Bus Plan (Gross Profit)	$ 205,160	(22,880)	(75,550)	(24,000)	82,730	(8,036)	(7,380)	$ 67,314
Cum Sales Plan vs Bus Plan (Gross Profit)	$ 205,160	182,280	106,730	82,730	82,730	74,694	67,314	$ 67,314
Budgeted % Gross Margin	41.8%	41.8%	41.8%	41.8%	41.8%	41.8%	41.8%	41.8%
Projected % Gross Margin	40.9%	42.4%	42.7%	40.0%	41.1%	41.8%	41.8%	41.2%

Cash Flow Planning

Cash flow planning can also be driven by the sales and operations plan. Cash flow projections cover both cash disbursements and cash receipts. Cash disbursements can be calculated for the material, direct labor, and variable overhead expenses. These cash disbursements can be combined with other financial numbers to develop a more complete cash flow projection for the company.

While the easiest way to produce cash flow projections is to base them on S&OP data, in some circumstances it will be more accurate to use all the detail data – purchase orders, master schedules, material and capacity plans, etc. – extended by the appropriate financial factors. If the detailed data can be updated quickly – nearly instantly – and the horizon for detailed planning is as long as the S&OP horizon, this may be better approach. However, in a typical company, the time required to update the detailed plans is significant and requires a signed off S&OP – just the thing being validated by the financial projections. In addition, the MPS horizon is typically much shorter than the S&OP horizon, meaning that the projections based on the MPS may cut off after three to six months, where the S&OP based projection would extend out eighteen months minimum.

Consequently, most companies use some type of summary projection of cash flow:

- Expenses for purchased material can be calculated by extending the aggregate supply plan from the sales and operations plan by the average material cost for products in the family. To develop a cash flow projection for purchased material, these material costs would be adjusted by the payables cycle – 15, 20, 30, 45 days. For example, if the payables cycle is thirty days, then the purchase dollars would be offset by thirty days to reflect the proper timing of the cash disbursements.

- Direct labor expense can be calculated in a similar way, since direct labor expense varies directly with levels of supply. In the simplest method, direct labor expense would be calculated from the supply plan from S&OP, and average labor costs offset by the payroll cycle.

    A slightly more detailed projection could be done using rough-cut capacity planning. Rough-cut capacity planning could be done for labor resources and load profiles that contain the number of standard hours per unit required to meet the supply plan. These standard hours would be converted to man-hours using the work center efficiency and accounting for breaks and lunch, and the man-hours summarized by labor grade and extended by the labor rate to project payroll expense. Projected overtime expense could be estimated by taking the labor hours above the normal work center capacity, summarizing them by labor grade and extending them by the overtime labor rates.

- The same methods could be used for calculating variable overhead expenses. Variable overhead expenses are those overhead expenses that vary directly with levels of supply. For example, the cost of electricity to run screw machines is a variable overhead expense; it varies based on the number of hours the screw machines run. Similarly in a company producing chemicals, the cost of electricity to run mixers and reactors would be a variable overhead expense. The cost of the natural gas required to run the heat treat furnaces or curing ovens would be another variable overhead expense.

- To calculate variable overhead expense, it would be necessary to have some rates like the cost of electricity per hour on the automatic screw machines, the cost of natural gas per hour on the heat treat furnaces, etc. These rates would then be extended by either the supply plan in S&OP or by the rough-cut capacity requirements for the resource center to give the projected variable overhead costs.

- Cash receipts can be projected from the appropriate shipping numbers in the S&OP. For example, in a make-to-order company, the supply plan in S&OP is the schedule of shipments. Scheduled completions would be extended by the selling price, or interplant transfer price, to give the projected billings.

  In a make-to-stock business, completions in the supply plan represent transfers to stock, not shipments. In general, the sales forecast is also the projection of shipments. (The only exception would be a situation where the master production schedule plus existing inventory doesn't satisfy the forecast – which in and of itself is a problem that negates any financial projections.

  In other words, the projected shipments for a make-to-stock business are sales forecasts whenever the projected on-hand balance is not negative. Projected shipments are extended by the selling price to give projected billings. The dates of these billings can be adjusted by the receivables cycle to get a cash receipts projection.

72 SALES AND OPERATIONS PLANNING STANDARD SYSTEM

Finished Goods Inventory Investment Planning
The financial planning interface to S&OP should provide a way to develop both the present value of finished goods inventory[22] and the projected value of finished goods inventory in the future. The present inventory value represents the value of the finished goods inventory in the stockroom and warehouses. The projected value of finished goods inventory is a projection of the inventory that will be on hand at the end of each month covered by the sales and operations plan.

The inventory projections coming out of sales and operations planning are limited to products that are make-to-stock and their finished goods inventory (or in the case of products that are finished to order, a semi-finished inventory). The projection would not typically include component and purchased material inventory value since these are not directly part of the S&OP planning process.

As in the case of other financial projections, the simplest way to calculate the present and projected values of finished goods inventory is to base the calculations on S&OP data by family and an average unit cost factor by family. A more accurate calculation would be to use all the detailed data – on hand balance by item, work-in-process by item, customer orders and forecasts, master schedules in the future, etc. – extended by the unit cost data by item.

In a system capable of fast replanning and simulation of future results, basing the finished goods inventory calculations on the detailed data and also calculating component and purchased material inventory value would be the preferred method. Unfortunately, in most companies the amount of time required to adjust the MPS and do all the planning calculations is excessive, and the horizon too short to make this useful.

Consequently, most companies use some type of summary based projection, limited to finished goods inventory when they are checking financial projections as part of their S&OP process.

The present value of inventory can be calculated from the total finished goods inventory for the family of products multiplied by the average unit cost. The projected inventory value can be calculated from the projected inventory at the

---

[22] In the case of families of products that are finish-to-order, there will be no "finished goods" inventory, but the software can project semi-finished inventory levels.

Chapter 6 Feeding Financial Analysis 73

end of each S&OP. The projected inventory, by month, from the S&OP system would be extended by the average unit costs to give the projected value of finished goods inventory.

Figure 6 – 2 below shows a typical dollarized sales and operations plan with cumulative totals. This report includes budget data, a simple cash flow projection, and a finished goods inventory projection.

In the example, four different categories of time phased information are shown:

Business plan performance in sales dollars
Sales plan performance – actual and planned – in sales dollars
Supply plan performance - actual and planned – in cost dollars
Finished goods inventory performance – actual and planned – in cost dollars

The column "Current Year Expected Results" shows projected performance through the end of the current fiscal year. Columns to the right show the latest projections for the next fiscal year.

Figure 6 – 2
Simple Cash Flow and Inventory Projection

Family:	All Families	Average Selling Price:	$ 1.960							
Description:	All Widgets	Standard Product Cost:	$ 1.140							

ALL FIGURES IN US DOLLARS		History			Year To Date	Current		Current Year	Next Year		
	JAN - JUL TOTAL	AUG	SEP	OCT	Results	NOV	DEC	Expected Results	JAN	FEB	MAR
Business Plan (Budgeted Sales Dollars)											
Budgeted Sales Plan	$ 2,802,800	392,000	450,800	411,600	$ 4,057,200	411,600	431,200	$ 4,900,000	459,620	484,316	621,516
Current Sales Plan	$ 3,365,920	332,640	264,670	370,500	$ 4,333,730	392,392	413,560	$ 5,139,682	459,620	484,316	621,516
Difference	$ 563,120	(59,360)	(186,130)	(41,100)	$ 276,530	(19,208)	(17,640)	$ 239,682	0	0	0
Cum Difference	$ 563,120	503,760	317,630	276,530	$ 276,530	257,322	239,682	$ 239,682	0	0	0
Sales (Sales Dollars)											
Last Sales Plan	$ 3,169,712	384,160	444,528	392,000	$ 4,390,400	411,600	431,200	$ 5,233,200	470,400	490,000	627,200
Current Sales Plan	$ 3,365,920	332,640	264,670	370,500	$ 4,333,730	392,392	413,560	$ 5,139,682	459,620	484,316	621,516
Actual Sales	$ 3,365,920	332,640	264,670	370,500	$ 4,333,730						
Difference	$ 196,208	(51,520)	(179,858)	(21,500)	$ (56,670)	(19,208)	(17,640)	$ (93,518)	(10,780)	(5,684)	(5,684)
Cum Difference	$ 196,208	144,688	(35,170)	(56,670)	$ (56,670)	(75,878)	(93,518)	$ (93,518)	(10,780)	(16,464)	(22,148)
Supply (Cost Dollars)											
Budgeted Supply	$ 1,729,608	223,440	258,552	228,000	$ 2,439,600	199,500	205,200	$ 2,844,300	245,100	324,900	359,100
Current Supply Plan	$ 1,428,420	239,400	167,580	239,400	$ 2,074,800	199,500	199,500	$ 2,473,800	239,400	319,200	359,100
Difference	$ (301,188)	15,960	(90,972)	11,400	$ (364,800)	0	(5,700)	$ (370,500)	(5,700)	(5,700)	0
Cum Difference	$ (301,188)	(285,228)	(376,200)	(364,800)	$ (364,800)	(364,800)	(370,500)	$ (370,500)	(5,700)	(11,400)	(11,400)
Finished Goods Inventory (Cost Dollars)											
Budget	$ 914,508	909,948	906,300	894,900	$ 894,900	855,000	809,400	$ 809,400	787,170	830,376	827,982
Plan	$ 352,032	255,360	303,240	319,200	$ 319,200	279,300	233,700	$ 233,700	205,200	245,100	239,400
Difference	$ (562,476)	(654,588)	(603,060)	(575,700)	$ (575,700)	(575,700)	(575,700)	$ (575,700)	(581,970)	(585,276)	(588,582)

Capital Planning

The financial planning interface to S&OP should support the capital planning processes of the business, in those cases where the capital investments have to do with production resources in support of the sales and operations plan. What this really means is that the supply and sales plans should be input to the capital planning and justification process. Decisions on capital need to be made in light of the most current product volumes.

Chapter 7
Measures of Performance

Reviewing key performance indicators is an important part of any working S&OP process. Experience suggests a set of standardized measurements (sometimes called *key performance indicators-KPI's* or *vital signs*) that should be published during the process, and reviewed at the meetings that make up the process. Some performance indicators will be reviewed in the early steps of the S&OP process, but not at the executive meeting. The *critical* metrics will be reviewed in the executive meeting.

Vital signs reviewed during the S&OP process:

- Measure whether the needs of customers are being met (on-time and in-full).
- Measure whether the financial objectives of the business as defined by the business plan are being met.
- Identify problems and then assist in prioritizing problems so they can be solved.
- Provide a scorecard for monitoring improvement.

The sales and operations planning system should include capabilities to capture and report the following:

1. Customer service performance by family and overall
    Customer delivery performance (on-time and in-full – OTIF) to request date
    Customer delivery performance (on-time and in-full) to promised date

2. Performance to budget (dollars) by family and overall
    Latest sales plan vs. budget dollars
    Profit projections for year
    Inventory versus budget dollars

3. Performance to plan (units) by family
    Actual shipments versus plan typically expressed as percentage attainment.
    Actual sales versus forecast (some measurement of accuracy or variability) typically expressed as attainment, percentage error, or mean absolute percentage error.

Actual supply versus supply plan expressed as percentage attainment, or percent variability from plan.
Actual inventory versus inventory plan (make-to-stock products) expressed as a percentage.
Actual backlog versus backlog plan (make-to-order products) expressed as a percentage.

The way these are actually reported will vary from company to company. In nearly every company, the "performance to plan" metrics will be reviewed as part of the family by family review, so summarizing them to a scorecard is somewhat redundant. For example, Figure 7 – 1 shows common performance to plan metrics displayed as part of the S&OP display itself. Metrics on this make-to-stock example show actual sales to budget, actual sales to plan, actual production to plan, and actual inventory to plan expressed as a percentage of the budget or plan for the period. (The formulas used to calculate these metrics are explained below as part of the general discussion of measurements.)

Figure 7 – 1
S&OP with Typical Performance to Plan Metrics

CALENDAR	CUM	History AUG	History SEP	History OCT	Year-to-Date Planned	Current NOV	Current DEC	Current Year Planned	Next Year JAN	Next Year FEB	Next Year MAR
ANNUAL OPERATING PLAN					Year-to-Date YTD Results			Current Year Expected Results			
Budgeted Sales	14300	2000	2300	2100	20700	2100	2200	25000	2345	2471	3171
Perf to Budget	17440	1680	1330	1950	22400	2002	2110	26512			
Cum Diff Perf to Budget	3140	2820	1850	1700	1700	1602	1512	1512			
SALES	CUM				YTD Results			Expected Results			
Last Sales Plan	16172	1960	2268	2000	22400	2100	2200	26700	2400	2500	3200
Current Sales Plan	17440	1680	1330	1950	22400	2002	2110	26512	2345	2471	3171
Actual Sales	17440	1680	1330	1950	22400						
Difference	1268	-280	-938	-50							
Curr as % of Last Sales Plan	108%	86%	59%	98%	100%	95%	96%	99%			
Cum Difference	1268	988	50	0							
SHIPMENTS	CUM				YTD Results			Expected Results			
Customer Orders by Promised Date	17440	1680	1330	1950	22400			26512			
Actual Shipments	17440	1680	1330	1950	22400						
SUPPLY	CUM				YTD Results			Expected Results			
Last Supply Plan	12110	1960	2268	2000	18338	1750	1800	21888	2150	2850	3150
Current Supply Plan	12530	2100	1470	2100	18200	1750	1750	21700	2100	2800	3150
Actual Supply	12530	2100	1470	2100	18200						
Difference	420	140	-798	100	-138						
Curr as % of Last Plan	103%	107%	65%	105%	99%	100%	97%	99%			
Cum Difference	420	560	-238	-138	-138						
INVENTORY					YTD Results			Expected Results			
Last Inventory Plan	3088	2240	2660	2800	2800	2450	2050	2050	1800	2150	2100
Current Inventory Plan	2240	2660	2800	2950	2950	2698	2338	2338	2093	2422	2401
Actual	2240	2660	2800	2950	2950						
Difference	-848	420	140	150	150						
Curr as % of Last Plan	73%	119%	105%	105%	105%	110%	114%	114%			

Even though some metrics are part of the family by family review, some companies like to have a summary scorecard that highlights overall and family by family performance. Often this would be reviewed first during the partnership and executive meetings. Other companies prefer to have an overall scorecard (summary statistics only) and a scorecard for each family.

Since in many companies the executive review of the sales and operations plan itself is "by exception", not every family will be reviewed in detail. The scorecard by family is a quick reference to current performance for each family.

In the end, each company needs to decide what kind of reporting makes the most sense for it. The important thing isn't the number of reports or displays or their formats, the important thing is that performance review of the vital signs is part of the S&OP process.

There may be other key performance indicators that are reviewed in the five step S&OP process. These additional metrics include:

- Actual supply versus MPS or finishing schedule
- Schedule stability
- Supplier performance
- Master production schedule versus supply plan

In some cases, these will be reviewed in the earlier steps and not in the executive meeting. In cases where executive management considers them critical, they will be reviewed in the executive meeting as well – or they will be part of the reference data provided but not formally reviewed.

How to Measure

Generally speaking, any measurement requires a sample, a tolerance, and a standard. The samples define what data is used for the measurement and may be taken differently depending upon the specific measurement. In some cases, the sample used for performance measurement could be based on random selection. In other cases, the sample could be all of the activities occurring during a specific period of time. In all of the vital signs described below the sample size covers all the events or data points during the period of time being measured.

Performance measurements must have reasonable tolerances. For example, on-time performance for a supplier might be defined as "delivered on the due date *plus or minus 1 day* and *plus or minus five percent of the order quantity*. In this case, the tolerance of "plus or minus 1 day" indicates that an order can be delivered a day late or a day early and still be considered on time. The tolerance of plus or minus five percent of the order quantity indicates that the quantity delivered can be delivered for slightly more or slightly less than that ordered and still be "in-full". Notice that this example may not be valid for your company – it may well be that for your kind of business, plus or minus 1 hour is the appropriate tolerance for time, and plus or minus zero is the appropriate tolerance for the quantity. The issue is not whether there should be tolerances, but what an appropriate and reasonable tolerance would be.

Finally, each measurement should have a performance standard or objective that it can be compared against. For example, good performance against an "on-time in-full against requested date" measurement, for some companies, would be 99%: Ninety-nine percent of all orders should be delivered on-time and in-full. For other companies serving different customers, selling into different markets, good OTIF performance might be 95%: ninety-five percent of all orders delivered on-time and in-full.

Customer Delivery Performance (OTIF) Against the Request Date

Each company must define the minimum acceptable customer delivery performance against the customer requested date. This is the percentage of the orders scheduled for delivery during a time period that must actually be delivered on time and in-full to the date requested.

> **Customer delivery performance to request date = number of orders delivered in-full to the requested date / number of orders requested**

Note that this is an *order fill rate* measurement based on the number of orders where every line item on the order was filled on-time. As such it is stricter than the common alternative, a *line item fill rate* which measures the percentage of line items that were filled on-time.

It is also a *delivery* measurement based on the orders that were actually delivered on time. The alternative, customer shipment performance, measures the percentage of orders that were shipped on-time and may not reflect whether the customer is being satisfied.

Finally this metric reflects the performance against the date that the customer requested, not the date the order was promised for delivery. This is the strictest, most "customer-centric" of all the typical measurements of customer service performance.

In most cases, the tolerance used in determining whether an order is on time will range from zero to several days; the "in-full" tolerance will typically range from 0 to 5%.

Customer Delivery Performance (OTIF) Against the Promised Date
The minimum acceptable customer delivery performance against the promised date is 99%. Ninety-nine percent of all customer orders scheduled for delivery during a time period must actually be delivered on-time and in-full against the promise that was made to the customer.

> Customer delivery performance to promised date = number of orders delivered in-full to the promised date / number of orders promised

Note that this, like the metric above, is an *order fill rate* measurement based on the number of orders where every line item on the order was filled on-time and in-full. As such it is stricter than one of the most common alternatives, a *line item fill rate* which measures the percentage of line items that were filled on-time.

It is also a *delivery* measurement based on the orders that were actually delivered on time against the promise. The alternative, customer shipment performance, measures the percentage of orders that were shipped on-time and may not reflect whether the customer is being satisfied.

In most cases, the tolerance used in determining whether an order is on time will range from zero to several days; the "in-full" tolerance will typically range from 0 to 5%.

Latest Plans Versus Budget Dollars Year-To-Date
The actual sales year-to-date should be compared against the budgeted revenue dollars for the same period. Similarly, the actual profit year-to-date should be compared to the budgeted profit for the same period.

Revenue and Profit Projections
Revenue dollars based on actual sales year-to-date plus the sales plan though the end of the fiscal year should be calculated and compared to budgeted revenue dollars for the year. Profit based on actuals year-to-date plus projections based on the sales plan through the end of the fiscal year should be calculated and compared to budgeted profit for the year.

Inventory Versus Budget Dollars
Current actual inventory be compared to budgeted inventory dollars.

Inventory performance = actual inventory dollars / budgeted or target inventory dollars

Actual Shipments Versus Scheduled Shipments

Minimum acceptable shipment performance is 99%. Ninety-nine percent of the shipment volume was actually shipped in the period scheduled.

Shipment performance = quantity shipped / quantity scheduled to be shipped

Actual Sales Versus Forecast (some measurement of accuracy or variability)

Demand variability is a function of the specific customers and the markets being serviced. As a result this is one of the standards that must set on a company by company basis. One company might think that outstanding performance was 79% of the forecasted demand (+/- 21% variability), where another might feel that 92% (+/- 8% variability) was achievable and the standard to measure against.

Generally speaking, companies measuring demand variability express it as a percentage, measured at the family level, either as attainment or variability. Attainment is measured as:

Sales attainment = actual sales / sales plan

Demand variability is typically measured in either of two ways:

Demand variability = (actual sales − sales plan) / sales plan

Or

Demand variability = (actual sales − sales plan) / actual sales

In the case of the variability measurements, the two formulas measure the "accuracy" of the volume forecasts, but don't indicate how much variability actually exists in the mix. For this reason, some companies prefer metrics that measure the average error considering the mix. This is called the mean absolute percentage error, and it is the sum of the individual errors across all items in the family:

$\text{MAPE} = \sum |(\text{actual sales} - \text{forecast})| / \sum (\text{actual sales})$

Actual Versus Supply Plan

The minimum supply plan performance ranges from +/-2% to +/-5% by family. Overall, aggregated performance across all product families should be within 2% of the agreed plan.

Typically the way this measurement is made is as follows:

> Supply plan performance for a period = (Actual volume produced − supply plan)/ supply plan

Typically this metric is reported as a percentage.

Actual Inventory Versus Inventory Plan (MTS and FTO)

Inventory variability is a composite measurement: it is a byproduct of supply plan and shipment plan performance. As such, "good performance" will vary from company to company.

One way to express inventory performance is as a variability measurement:

> Inventory variability = (planned inventory − actual inventory) divided by planned inventory.

Typically this metric is reported as a percentage.

Actual Backlog Versus Backlog Plan (MTO and FTO)

Backlog variability is also a composite measurement: it is a byproduct of sales plan and shipment plan performance. As such, "good performance" against the backlog target will vary from company to company.

One way to express backlog performance is as a variability measurement done by period:

> Backlog variability = (planned backlog − actual backlog) divided by planned backlog.

Typically this metric is reported as a percentage.

Actual Supply Versus MPS (or Finishing Schedule)

The master schedule performance needed to support an effective sales and operations planning process is 95%. Ninety-five percent of all master schedule orders scheduled during a time period must be produced and delivered on time. In most cases, the tolerance used in determining whether an order is on time will range from zero to several days.

One typical way to express MPS performance is:

> MPS performance = (Number of MPS orders produced on time) / Number of MPS orders scheduled

Schedule Stability

The schedule stability metric is really a diagnostic metric to measure and display the amount of change occurring to the master schedule – and by extension – to the entire supporting supply chain. This can be helpful in two ways:

- As a way to relate the volume of changes to on-time delivery performance – it may be that there is a direct relationship between lots of changes and missed deliveries.
- As a way to focus improvement efforts on increased flexibility. In other words by knowing how much flexibility to change the supply chain can accommodate, it may be possible to focus improvements in a way that this flexibility is increased.

Normally a company will measure the number of changes to the schedule, or the percentage of the schedule that is changing, within each time zone used to manage change to the schedules

> Schedule stability = number of MPS orders that changed

Or

> Schedule stability = number of MPS orders that changed / number of MPS orders in the period

Supplier On-Time Performance

The supplier on-time performance needed to support an effective sales and operations planning process is 95%. Ninety-five percent of all supplier deliveries scheduled during a time period must be delivered on-time and for the full quantity. In most cases, the tolerance used in determining whether an order is on-time will range from zero to several days, and the in-full tolerance might be 5%. In some extreme circumstances, the tolerance might be "within the same week" – any orders delivered in the week scheduled (which might be as much as four days early or late) would be on-time.

> Supplier on-time performance = (Number of orders delivered on-time) / Number of MPS deliveries scheduled

Master Production Schedule Versus Supply Plan

The sum of the master production schedules for all items within a family should be within 5% of the supply plan for the period. As explained in chapter 3, the sum over multiple periods should trend to zero.

This is a measurement over current and future time periods.

PART 4:
GRAPHICAL DISPLAYS

Chapter 8
Graphical Displays of S&OP Data

The prior chapters were concerned with the basic functionality and reporting that is part of a normal S&OP process. This chapter looks at the alternative of presenting S&OP data in graphical form, and explains how graphical displays of the numeric data can be organized to support the decision-making process.

Generally speaking, a well-designed S&OP system will not only have the correct data and calculations, it will also present it in a well-organized and readable set of data displays. This is all part of a general concept of "human engineering" in software. Good human engineering often makes the difference between a system that's difficult to use and one that's uncomplicated, easy to understand, and simple to operate effectively.

Increasingly, companies using S&OP are turning to graphical displays of the data to improve the human engineering of the system even more and to augment the tabular, spreadsheet-like displays that displays the detailed data. Since nearly all the S&OP data – time phased planning, performance to budget, performance to plan, vital signs, historical performance and future projections – are candidates for graphing, this chapter is primarily about why and how to develop graphs that work, not what to graph.

What Is Motivating Companies to Use Graphs in S&OP?
Here are some of the reasons that companies are using graphical displays of numeric data for S&OP:

- To present complex data with the kind of clarity not typically possible with displays of raw tabular data - in other words, to make large amounts of data coherent, to draw out the information content often hidden among the numbers, and to do it in the shortest time and the smallest space.
- To stimulate thinking about the data and what is revealed by it. Edward Tufte[23], perhaps the best-known researcher into the graphical display of data,

---

[23] Edward Tufte authored four books on the subject of graphical display of numeric data. The first book "The Visual Display of Quantitative Information", Graphics Press, Cheshire CT was named on of the "100 Best Non-fiction Books of the Twentieth Century". Anyone designing graphical displays of S&OP data should read Tufte's books.

said "...effective analytic designs entail turning thinking principles into seeing principles". (It could also be said that effective analytic designs turn thinking into seeing into thinking.)
- To make the main trends visible at a glance – allowing the users to focus on important business issues without "drowning in the data".
- To encourage comparisons of data, that would be difficult to do from raw data.
- To impart a common understanding of business conditions to all S&OP participants irrespective of their language, culture, or gender, and to do it without any assumptions about advanced training in research methods or statistics.
- To engage and focus executive management on the significant problems and issues of the business, in the shortest possible time. To keep extraneous data and "busy" spreadsheet displays from unnecessarily consuming time in the executive S&OP meeting.
- To show variability and uncertainty in performance as revealed by the data.
- To simplify the reporting and review process, particularly in step five (the executive S&OP meeting) of the S&OP process.

Michael Friendly of the Psychology Department at York University in Toronto says it well:

"Like good writing, good graphical displays of data communicate ideas with clarity, precision, and efficiency. Like poor writing, bad graphical displays distort or obscure the data, make it harder to understand or compare, or otherwise thwart the communicative effect which the graph should convey."

And Edward Tufte said:

"Graphics *reveal* data. Indeed graphics can be more precise and revealing than conventional statistical computations."

What Characterizes Well-designed Graphs?

Experience across a range of fields suggests that a well-designed graphical display[24] should:

---

[24] Points 4 through 11 adapted from
http://www.cochrane.dk/cochrane/handbook/appendices/appendix_8a._considerations_and_recommendations_for_figures_in_cochrane_reviews__graphs_of_statistical_data.htm

1. Present the key information in a convenient number of reports or displays. Replacing a single spreadsheet with fifteen pages of graphs is not progress by any standard. Less is more.

The objective is to make effective use of the people's time by concentrating on the problem conditions without forcing them to analyze the whole mass of current data.

2. Not be oversimplified. Don't dumb down the data and don't distort it with cute graphics. If the audience is smart enough to read S&OP spreadsheets, they are smart enough to read graphs of that data.

3. Provide "pegging" to the source. Often this means successively more detailed visual displays of the data.

5. Include clear labeling. Don't hide the scales, captions and labels. An effective graph should still be understandable without the data tables in the S&OP packet (although for a variety of reasons this would not be recommended since there is a significant amount of source data that will not be graphed).

6. When comparing two different graphs use the same scale on each one.

7. Avoid gridline overload – make sure gridlines don't interfere with the data itself.

8. Keep clutter to a minimum. Avoid poorly organized and cluttered formats. Some graphs try to fit too much information into too small a space, resulting in a confusing mass that serves to confuse not to inform. Reading this kind of graph may be an exercise in frustration as people are forced to switch back and forth between the different information.

An example of an S&OP graph that may border on being too cluttered, and consequently confusing, is an S&OP graph that tries to show all the different aspects of historical performance (budgeted and planned sales, planned and actual sales, planned and actual shipments, planned and actual supply, planned

---

and http://www.washington.edu/computing/training/560/zz-tufte.html#Intro

and actual inventory/backlog) and all the future projections (business plan, sales plan, shipments plan, supply plan, inventory or backlog plan) all in the same display. Jamming all this data into a single graph may be just too much information in too small a space. Even limiting the data to just primary sales, supply and inventory information, as in Figure 8 – 2 below, may border on information overload.

S&OP Graphical Displays

The following are typically candidates for graphical or visual displays:

- Key performance indicators (vital signs).
- Projected performance to budget (S&OP versus business plan)
- Past performance to plan (sales, shipments, production, inventory, backlog)
- Projected plans (sales versus production versus inventory for example)
- Rough-cut capacity planning data.

Some examples of these graphical displays are shown in Figures 8 – 1 though 8 – 5. Refer the source spreadsheet (Chapter 10) to see color versions of these displays.

Figure 8 – 1
Projected Performance to Annual Operating Plan

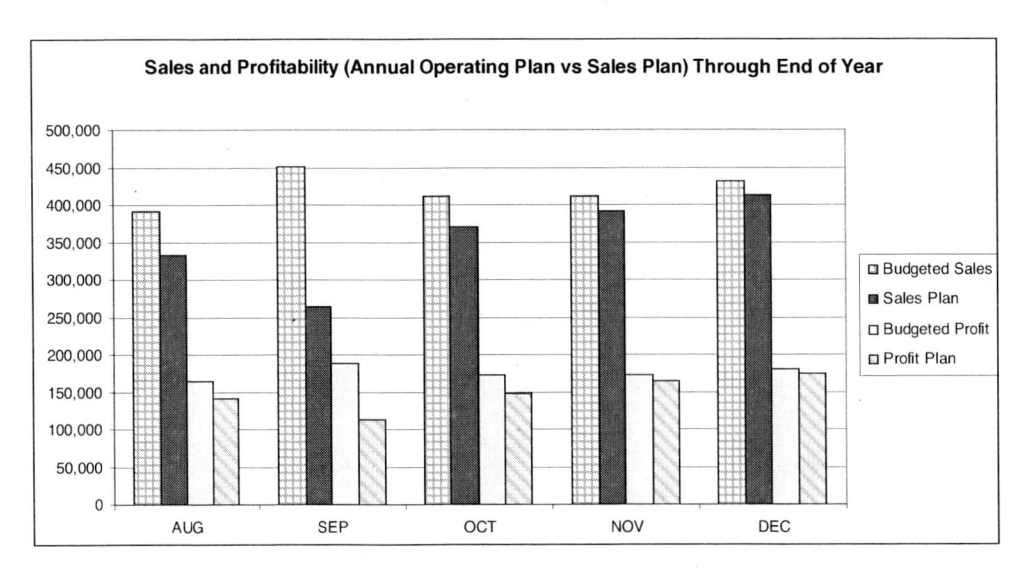

Chapter 8 Graphical Displays of Data 91

Figure 8 – 2
Historical and Projected Sales and Operations Plan (Units)

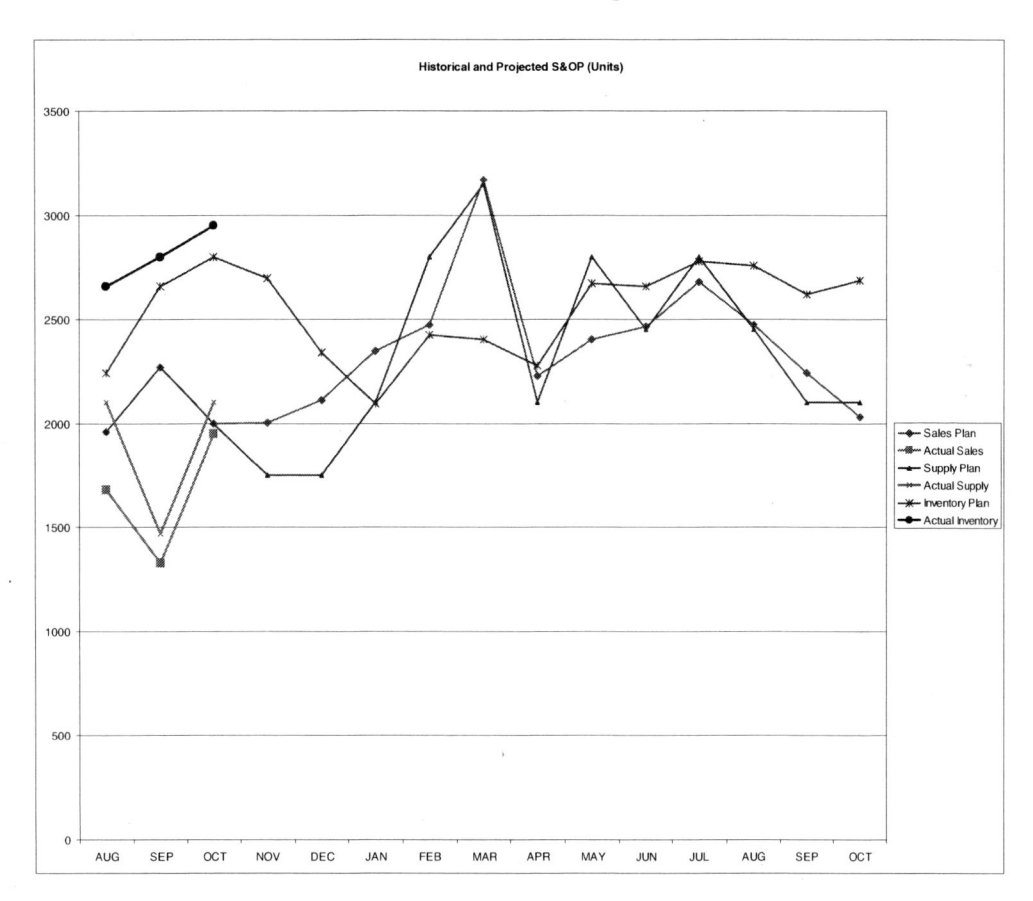

Figure 8 – 3
Sales and Operations Plan (No Actuals)

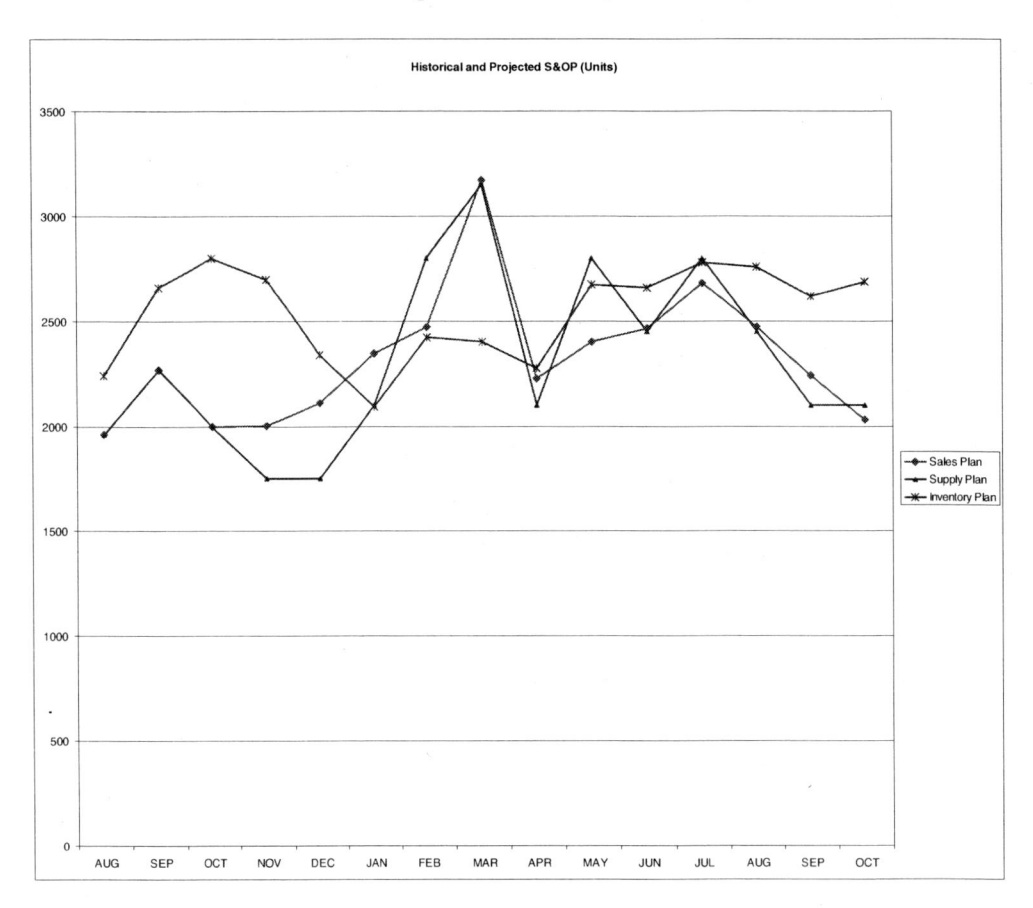

Figure 8 – 4
Sales and Operations Plan With Inventory Trend Line

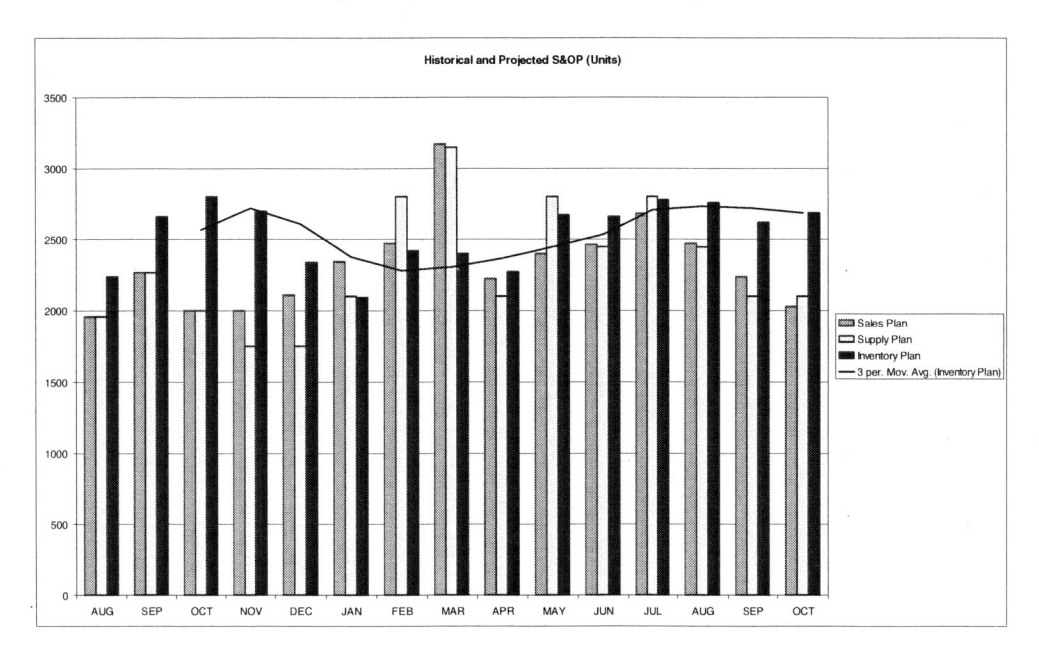

Figure 8 – 5
Rough-Cut Capacity Plan

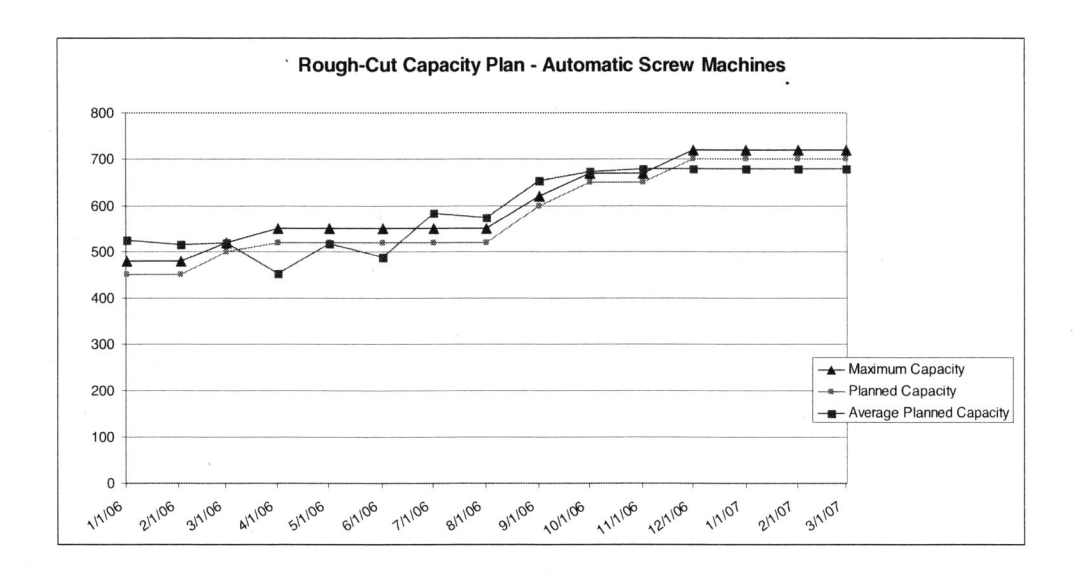

Each company should choose the graphical displays that are most helpful for them in achieving the overall goals of S&OP. For many companies the primary displays will probably focus on revenue and profit plan performance against the annual operating plan, on customer on-time delivery performance, and on future projections of the sales and operations plan (sales, production, inventory and backlog).

PART 5:
SUMMARY

Chapter 9
Functional Checklists

Sales and Operations Planning

Summary

Basic S&OP Data
Provide the basic data required to support the calculations, comparisons and conversions that are part of S&OP. Provide a transaction system for maintaining this data. Basic S&OP data includes:

1. Family data

    Product family identifier
    Description
    Type of family (MTS, MTO)
    Family group (for summarization)
    Customer lead time
    Critical time fence
    Primary unit of measure
    Alternate units of measure (hours, kilos, tons, etc.)
    Conversion factors (factors to translate the S&OP in the standard unit of measure to the S&OP in an alternate unit).
    Average selling price(s)
    Average cost(s) of goods sold
       Cost of material
       Cost of direct labor
       Cost of burden
    Inventory target expressed as weeks of coverage
    Backlog target expressed as weeks of sales or shipments

2. Time phased data
    Planned sales (past and future periods)
    Actual sales (past periods only)
    Customer orders by ship date.
    Actual shipments (past periods only)
    Planned supply (past and future periods)
    Actual supply (past periods only)
    Planned backlog (both past and future periods)
    Actual backlog for past periods

Planned inventory (past and future periods)
Actual inventory for past periods
Target inventory
Target backlog

3. Planning bills of material or planning hierarchies
   Family to family (parent to component) relationship
   Quantity per

4. Calendar
   S&OP period start date
   Fiscal year for period
   Days in S&OP period
   Supply days in period
   Sales days in period
   Normal production time in period (for the takt time calculation)
   Temporary production time adjustments in period (for an operational takt time calculation)

5. Commentary
   Text of manufacturing assumptions by family and date
   Text of sales assumptions by family and date
   Text of explanations of deviations in past performance by family and date
   Text of anticipated impact of new product trials
   Text of planned actions and assignments

Fundamental S&OP Calculations:
Provide the basic calculation upon which S&OP is based:

Make-to-stock
The correct basic calculation for a make-to-stock family is:

$$\text{Ending inventory} = \text{Beginning inventory} + \text{supply} - \text{shipments}$$

Make-to-order
The correct basic calculation for a make-to-order family is:

$$\text{Ending backlog} = \text{Beginning backlog} + \text{bookings} - \text{shipments}$$

Mixed or finish-to-order

The correct calculations for a mixed MTS/MTO family or for a finish-to-order family are:

Ending inventory = starting inventory − the shipping plan + the supply plan

Ending backlog = starting backlog + the sales plan − the shipping plan

Basic S&OP Displays

Provide a sales and operations planning display showing key planning information as well as comparisons of plans to actual performance. This would typically include:

Historical data, minimum 3 months past, in monthly buckets
    Planned sales
    Actual sales or bookings
    Customer orders by promised ship date
    Actual shipments
    Planned supply
    Actual supply
    Planned inventory (make-to-stock)
    Actual inventory (make-to-stock)
    Planned backlog (make-to-order)
    Actual backlog (make-to-order)

Current and Future, minimum 18 months future, in monthly buckets
    Planned sales
    Planned shipments (required only for mixed or finish-to-order families)
    Customer orders by promised ship date
    Planned supply
    Planned inventory
    Planned backlog

Provide an S&OP reporting horizon that extends beyond the master scheduling horizon. Normally the S&OP horizon would be 18 months.

Provide reporting alternatives that allow the user to:

View the impact on the inventory and backlog plan based on the current sales plan and supply plan. This is the primary S&OP report used for evaluating, reviewing, adjusting and creating the final approved sales and operations plan.

View the impact on the supply plan when the sales plan is updated and the inventory or backlog are fixed. This is an auxiliary S&OP report primarily used for simulating production alternatives.

Provide a way to store the last sales plan and the last supply plan, along with the ability to show the last plans versus the current plans. This may include computing and displaying the difference between the last plan and the current plan, either in units or as a percentage difference.

Provide a mechanism to store multiple prior versions of the Sales and Operations Plan. This mechanism might store the prior plan anytime the plan changes, or it might simply be an archiving mechanism to store the S&OP spreadsheets (perhaps along with agendas and meeting minutes) after the completion of each S&OP cycle (monthly).

Provide the calculations to convert projected inventory quantities to weeks or months of coverage and inventory turnover and display it as part of the S&OP time phased data.

Provide the calculations to convert projected backlog quantities to weeks or months of backlog and display it as part of the S&OP time phased data.

Provide a way to project the target inventory based on "desired days, weeks or months of coverage". Provide a way to maintain the inventory target by month.

Provide a way to project the target backlog based on "desired days weeks or months of backlog". Provide a way to maintain the backlog target by month.

Provide the calculations to convert sales plans to the sales rate per day and the supply plan to the supply rate per day.

Calculate and display takt time and operational takt time for comparison to designed cycle times.

Provide a mechanism to compare the supply plan to the summarized master production schedule.

Provide a way to estimate high and low sales plan limits and assess their impact on inventory or backlog.

Provide a mechanism to convert the sales and operations plans from the primary unit of measure to units of measure meaningful to finance, manufacturing, engineering, sales and marketing, etc.

Provide a method, to be used when required, to convert marketing families into manufacturing families, or vice versa. (Normally this would not be required, since a single set of families would be used for sales planning and supply planning. However in those situations where sales planning is done in marketing oriented groups and supply planning is done in manufacturing groups, this function helps with the translation of data back and forth.)

Provide a way to aggregate data into higher level groupings. This would include a way to aggregate item data into family or subfamily groupings, subfamilies into families, and families into higher level business groupings, and a way to summarize sales and operations planning data into divisional or corporate totals.

Rough-Cut Planning

Summary

Rough-cut Planning Basic Data
Provide the basic data required to support the calculations, comparisons and conversions that are part of rough-cut planning. Provide a transaction system for maintaining this data. Basic rough-cut data includes:

1. Key resources for rough-cut capacity planning
   Resource identifier
   Description
   Type of resource (capacity or material)
   Driver (driven by supply plan, driven by sales plan, driven by inventory plan)
   Unit of measure (standard hours, tons, minutes, days, etc. for rough-cut capacity planning, material unit of measure for rough-cut material planning)
   Actual demonstrated capacity
   Planned demonstrated capacity data
   Maximum capacity data

2. Time phased capacity data
   Resource identifier
   Period
   Planned demonstrated capacity data for the period
   Maximum capacity data for the period

3. Load profiles (representative routings or bill of resources) for rough-cut planning
   Family identifier
   Resource identifier
   Quantity required (quantity per unit of family)
   Offset weeks or months

Provide a mechanism for capturing actual demonstrated capacity.

Where necessary, provide the detailed data behind actual and planned demonstrated and maximum capacities. This might include current and planned productivity, current and planned shift patterns, hours per shift, planned downtime, planned overtime, etc. These factors should be used in the calculation of planned and maximum capacity by period.

Where routing standards vary significantly from item to item, provide a way to estimate the load profile quantity per based on a weighted average calculation that takes into account the standard run time and the item's contribution to total production volume.

Rough-cut calculations

Explode the sales and operations plan through the load profiles to calculate rough-cut requirements for each resource. Adjust the date of these requirements by the offset time. Summarize by month into rough-cut requirements in total for the resource.

Distinguish resources that are handled differently in rough-cut planning (production resources driven by the supply plan, sales resources driven by the sales plan, shipping or finishing resources driven by the shipping plan, inventory resources driven from the inventory plan):

Calculate rough-cut capacity plans for resources affected by supply volumes, for resources affected by sales volumes, for resources affected by shipping (finishing) volumes, and for resources affected by inventory (or backlog) levels using the appropriate planning data from S&OP.

Provide a way to calculate future planned demonstrated capacity based on actual demonstrated and future planned adjustments (number of people or equipment, overtime, changes to shift patterns, changing productivity, etc.).

Rough-cut Planning Basic Reporting

Provide a summary rough-cut capacity planning report displaying the total capacity required for each period and the capacity available in the period. This display should include:

> Rough-cut capacity planning displays show required capacity as well as a rolling 3 month average capacity requirement.
>
> A comparison of capacity required to the actual and planned demonstrated capacity and maximum capacity. Calculate and display the percentage capacity utilization as part of the rough-cut capacity plan.

Provide a summary rough-cut material planning report for each critical material, displaying the total material required for each period.

Provide pegging displays showing the details of the rough-cut planning process. This report would show which family or families had sales and operations plans causing the rough-cut requirements in each time period.

Financial Planning

Summary

Basic Financial Planning Integration
Provide functions to support:

- Budgeting and business planning for future years.
- Projecting current year revenue, margin, and profit based on current sales plans and forecasts, and actual performance to date during the year.
- Reconciling revenue plans, targets and budgets from the business plan to current operational projections.
- Projecting future cash flows.
- Projecting inventory investment based upon future sales and supply levels, and planned or actual average cost of goods sold.
- Capital planning.

Provide a method to support a comparison of the S&OP against the business plan for the full (current) fiscal year. Business plan measurements show performance to date and projected sales against the budget.

Provide profitability projections based on year-to-date actuals and anticipated future performance. Worksheets should include profit by period and a projection forward through the end of the fiscal year.

Provide profit projections on an accumulated basis, by period, through the end of the fiscal year, and then reset and accumulated from the new fiscal year start date.

Calculate sales in dollars, euros, reals, or sterling, etc. – whether actual sales or projections – from demand and the appropriate selling price (average actual or anticipated average selling price). Calculate costs in dollars, euros, etc. using the appropriate cost of goods number (average actual or anticipated average COGS).

Track budgeted average selling price (ASP) and cost of goods (COGS) sold versus actual and current ASP and COGS

Provide a way to monitor margins – projected versus budget.

Performance Measurements

Summary

Basic Metrics and KPIs
Provide the following minimum KPIs and an appropriate sampling method:

Customer service performance by family and overall:
- Customer delivery performance (on-time and in-full – OTIF) to request date.
- Customer delivery performance (on-time and in-full) to promised date.

Performance to budget (dollars) by family and overall:
- Latest sales plan vs. budget dollars.
- Profit projections for year.
- Inventory versus budget dollars.

Performance to plan (units) by family:
- Actual shipments versus plan expressed as percentage attainment.
- Actual sales versus forecast (some measurement of accuracy or variability) typically expressed as attainment, percentage error or MAPE.
- Actual supply versus supply plan expressed as percentage attainment.
- Actual inventory versus inventory plan (make-to-stock products) expressed as a percentage.
- Actual backlog versus backlog plan (make-to-order products) expressed as a percentage.

Provide the following additional metrics:

Actual supply versus finishing schedule versus MPS.
Schedule stability.
Supplier performance.
Master production schedule versus supply plan.

Use reasonable tolerances wherever appropriate.

Report performance against agreed minimums and targets.

Graphical Displays of S&OP Data

Summary

S&OP Graphical Displays
Provide graphical displays of appropriate S&OP related data:

- Key performance indicators (vital signs).
- Projected performance to budget (S&OP versus business plan).
- Past performance to plan (sales, shipments, production, inventory, backlog).
- Projected plans (sales versus production versus inventory for example).
- Rough-cut capacity planning data.

PART 6:
REFERENCE SOFTWARE

Chapter 10
Reference Software Overview and Quick Start

The sales and operations planning software provided with this book was designed as reference software to help you understand the typical calculations of S&OP, rough-cut capacity planning and S&OP-based financial projections.

Please read the disclaimer in Appendix D before you open the software or install it on your own computer. Opening or installing the software will be interpreted as accepting the terms and conditions of the disclaimer.

If you purchased the Sales and Operations Planning Standard System directly from Gray Research or the Partners for Excellence, you may have also purchased a CD containing the reference software. If you purchased the book from a bookseller like Amazon, Barnes and Noble, Borders, or your local independent bookstore, you can download the latest version of the software from the Gray Research website:

http://www.grayresearch.com/sopdownload.htm

Even if you have the CD, you may want to go to the Gray Research website to download the latest version of the programs. Unfortunately, bugs do creep into software – a plus sign when it should be a minus or vice versa, an incorrect cell reference, etc. – all inadvertent but problems nonetheless. We've endeavored to keep the software as clean as possible, but no one writes perfect code. You can retrieve the most current version with corrections from reported problems at:

http://www.grayresearch.com/sopdownload.htm.

Create a new directory called eSOP on the C: drive of your computer and save the downloaded file (database.zip) there. Then unzip the files into the C:\eSOP directory.

You can also download a more extensive set of documentation using the link:

http://www.grayresearch.com/sop_software/sopdocumentation.htm

The reference software includes:

- The Excel worksheets used to generate the examples throughout the book. These are fully functional spreadsheets with the calculations needed to generate typical S&OP comparisons. Specifically, worksheets are provided for make-to-stock, make-to-order, and finish-to-order S&OP comparisons, and for rough-cut capacity planning. In the case of these worksheets, however, there are no data feeds from saved sales, production, inventory, backlog or capacity plans.

- A simple Access and Excel-based system (e-SOP) that includes data and some alternative formats for S&OP and the financial projections. The spreadsheets that are included here include logic to retrieve stored data from the Access database as well as many of the calculations for S&OP described in the book. These spreadsheets also demonstrate some different design decisions with respect to the format of the displays and how the calculations can be done.

  The e-SOP reference software includes preloaded data for families, resources, load profiles and S&OP data like forecasts, supply plans, inventory plans, etc. However, it also includes basic maintenance functionality so that you can add, change and delete data and model some of your own company information.

By understanding the functionality of the reference software you can reduce some of the software design and programming effort required to build your own system. Or you can use it to validate the functions and calculations of software you are purchasing, or have purchased for S&OP.

Because the reference software uses MS Excel for its reporting functions, you don't have to be a computer expert to understand how the calculations are being done. Most people who have used Excel for business analysis are more than qualified to understand the basic calculations embedded in the reference spreadsheets.

Quick Start:
You can open any of the spreadsheets that are part of the reference software directly from the CD or from the C:\eSOP directory where you saved the downloaded programs. First verify that you have Excel 2000 (or later) loaded on your computer. To open from the CD, place the S&OP Reference Software CD in your CD drive and open it. Open the "eSOP" folder and locate the following files:

MTO_format.xls
MTS_format.xls
FTO_format.xls

Rough_Cut_Formats.xls
MTS_Standard_eSOP.xls
MTO_Standard_eSOP.xls
RCCPAnalysis.xls

To open from the downloaded programs, open the c:/eSOP folder and locate the following files:

MTO_format.xls
MTS_format.xls
FTO_format.xls
Rough_Cut_Formats.xls
MTS_Standard_eSOP.xls
MTO_Standard_eSOP.xls
RCCPAnalysis.xls

You can open these files using MS Excel in the normal way. Regarding any messages you may receive during the process of opening these files this way, respond "enable macros" and "enable automatic refresh".

Alternative Quick Start
The eSOP Sales and Operations Planning software comes preloaded with data. You can test its functionality and review the functionality with the sample data simply by loading it to your computer and the selecting the appropriate function and family (or resource if you are testing the rough-cut capacity planning logic).

Follow these steps:

1a. Verify that you have Access 2000 loaded, and that when it was loaded, you selected the options for also loading DAO (data access objects). If you don't have DAO loaded, stop and do it now. The software will not run without DAO loaded.

1b. Verify that your system has the following file: msowcf.dll. If it doesn't, download it from the Internet and place it in your windows\system32 directory. Register it by selecting Start ... Run ... and then enter regsvr32 msowcf.dll. The software will not run without this file loaded to your system.

2. Create a directory: C:\eSOP.

3. Check for updates to the software – you can download the latest version of the reference software using the following link:

114 THE SALES AND OPERATIONS PLANNING STANDARD SYSTEM

http://www.grayresearch.com/sopdownload.htm

You can also download a more extensive set of documentation using the link:

http://www.grayresearch.com/sop_software/sopdocumentation.htm

Save the downloaded file (database.zip) to the C:\eSOP directory. Then unzip the files into the same directory.

Verify that you have the following files in the C:\eSOP directory:

eSOP.mdb - eSOP forms and menus
eSOP_be.mdb - the backend database
MTO_format.xls
MTS_format.xls
FTO_format.xls
Rough_Cut_Formats.xls
MTS_Standard_eSOP.xls
MTO_Standard_eSOP.xls
RCCPAnalysis.xls

4. If you did not download the latest version and are installing from a CD, extract the software from database.zip and load it to your C:\eSOP directory. Verify that you have the following files in the C:\eSOP directory:

eSOP.mdb - eSOP forms and menus
eSOP_be.mdb - the backend database
MTO_format.xls
MTS_format.xls
FTO_format.xls
Rough_Cut_Formats.xls
MTS_Standard_eSOP.xls
MTO_Standard_eSOP.xls
RCCPAnalysis.xls

5. Launch eSOP. You can do this by double clicking on eSOP.mdb or you can launch Access, select File ... Open and then select eSOP.mdb from the c:\eSOP directory. (To open the database without launching the menu system, select eSOP.mdb, hold the shift key down and hit enter. From there you can select "MainMenu" from among the forms and hit enter to launch the menu system.)

6. You will see a "splash screen" showing some information about Gray Research and the copyright notice. This will go away after a few seconds and be replaced by the menu system.

Basically the way the menu system works is this:

There are two distinct panes. The upper pane consists of the groups of functions that are included in the system. When you select from the upper pane (click on one of the entries), the actual functions appear in the bottom frame.

Select a function from the lower pane and click OK, and the system will launch the function. Experiment with navigation in the system.

7. Select "S&OP Standard Reference Formats" from the upper pane and then select "Make-to-Stock S&OP display" in the lower pane. Click on OK.

This will launch an Excel spreadsheet containing a make-to-stock S&OP format. This is the same spreadsheet used to generate the sample displays shown in the book. By hiding the appropriate rows in this spreadsheet, you should be able to duplicate the formats shown in chapters 2 – 4.

You can repeat this selection process to launch the other formats – a make-to-order format, a finish-to-order format, and a rough-cut capacity planning format.

Experiment with launching these reference displays. Review how the basic calculations are done in the different spreadsheets.

8. Review some of the alternate S&OP formats that are connected to data stored in the Access database. Launch the primary MTS S&OP spreadsheet, by selecting "Sales & Operations Planning – eSOP – Reporting Formats" in the upper pane and "MTS S&OP display – primary worksheet" in the lower pane.

This will launch the Excel function that displays the sales and operations planning data for a single family. (It's the primary format because it calculates the inventory plan from the sales and supply plans you'd loaded). It automatically refreshes the current date and adjusts all the cells to reflect the proper period date based on the current period start date stored in the control file.

The way you tell the system which family you'd like to see is this:
Select Tools ... Macro ... Macros and then choose "UpdateExternalData" and Run. The macro will prompt you for a group (enter **Opns001**) and then for a family (families numbered Family01 – Family04, and Family11 – Family13 are set

up as make-to-stock families). **Family01** has reasonably representative data. The macro will retrieve all the S&OP data for the family you select and display it in multiple worksheets. The ones that you probably be most interested in are the ones labeled "Sales and Operations Plan", "Financial Projection", and "Graphs".

You may also be interested in the way that the rough-cut capacity planning calculations are embedded in the workbook, with the primary projection of the capacity requirements just below the sales and operations plan, and one worksheet for each resource showing the time phased plan itself. This should give you some ideas about how to construct the calculations and displays within your own system.

If you want to change any of your S&OP data, go back to the Access functions of the system and select from the "Update Time Phased Data" group. Once you've updated the data in Access you can re-import it to the spreadsheet by rerunning the UpdateExternalData macro in the spreadsheet.

9. Launch the simulation MTS S&OP spreadsheet, by selecting "Sales & Operations Planning – eSOP – Reporting Formats" in the upper pane and "MTS S&OP display – simulation worksheet" in the lower pane.

This will launch the Excel function that displays the simulation sales and operations planning data for a single family. (It's a simulation oriented format because it calculates the supply plan from the sales and inventory plans you'd loaded. While this is not the principal way that someone would operate S&OP, there are times when knowing the supply impact of a fixed inventory plan can be helpful – for example, when there is a limitation on inventory storage space. In other situations it may be helpful to know the "optimal" supply plan based on a given level of inventory based on a customer service calculation). This version of the spreadsheet also automatically refreshes the current date and adjusts all the cells to reflect the proper period date based on the current date stored in the control file.

The way you tell the system which family you'd like to see is this:

Select Tools ... Macro ... Macros and then choose "UpdateExternalData" and Run. The macro will prompt you for an operations group (enter **Opns001**) and then for a family (families numbered Family01 – Family04, and Family11 – Family13 are set up as make-to-stock families). **Family01** has reasonably representative data. The macro will retrieve all the S&OP data for the family you select and display it in multiple worksheets. The ones that you will probably be most interested in are the ones labeled "Sales and Operations Plan", "Financial Projection", and "Graphs".

If you want to change any of your S&OP data, go back to the Access functions of the system and select from the "Update Time Phased Data" group. Once you've updated the data in Access you can reimport it to the spreadsheet by rerunning the UpdateExternalData macro in the spreadsheet.

10. Repeat steps 8 and 9 for the make-to-order S&OP formats. Here, enter **optns002** for the operations group, and select from Family05 – Family10 when prompted for the family. Families 05 -10 are set up with make-to-order data. **Family05** has reasonably representative data.

11. Run the rough-cut capacity plan: select "Batch processing functions" in the upper panel and "Capacity plan generation in the lower". Hit "OK". When this process is finished, a pop-up message box will appear. If you are literate in Visual Basic for Applications, you may want to review the program logic that generates the rough-cut plan. It can be found among the program modules in the Access database.

12. Launch the capacity planning spreadsheet RCCPAnalysis, by selecting "Capacity planning" in the upper pane and "Capacity analysis spreadsheet" for a single resource in the lower pane.

This will launch the Excel function that displays the rough-cut capacity planning data for a single resource.

The way you tell the system which resource or work center you'd like to see is this:

Select the first tab in the workbook. Enter the resource you'd like to see at the top of the sheet (you can enter any resource from MResource01 to MResource12, SResource01 to SResource06, IResource01 to IResource06. Try MResource01 or MResource02, and make sure that "cg" is loaded as the data source option. The macro will retrieve all the capacity planning data for the resource you've specified and display it in multiple worksheets. The ones that you will be most interested in are the ones labeled "Pegging" and "Capacity Plan".

13. If you want to change any of your S&OP data or capacity planning data, go back to the Access functions of the system and select from the "Maintain master data" to maintain family data, "Maintain planning data" group to update sales and

supply plans or other time phased data, or the capacity profiles associated with an S&OP family.

For example, select "Maintain master data" from the upper pane and then select "Update Family Master" in the lower pane. Click on OK.

Once the maintenance screen appears, look in the upper right hand corner for a "pull down" selection box labeled "Find family:". Click on the down arrow and select "Widgets" from the pull down list. You may have to use the slider to advance to Widgets in this list of families.

All the maintenance functions work basically like this, although sometimes the pull down list is families, sometimes resources, sometimes dates, etc.

14. Now experiment with the other functionality in the system.

Chapter 11
Reference Software Basic UI and Functionality

Organization

The e-SOP Reference Software provides a simple user interface based on a menu and submenu.

When you launch the e-SOP Reference Software, a menu similar to the one below appears:

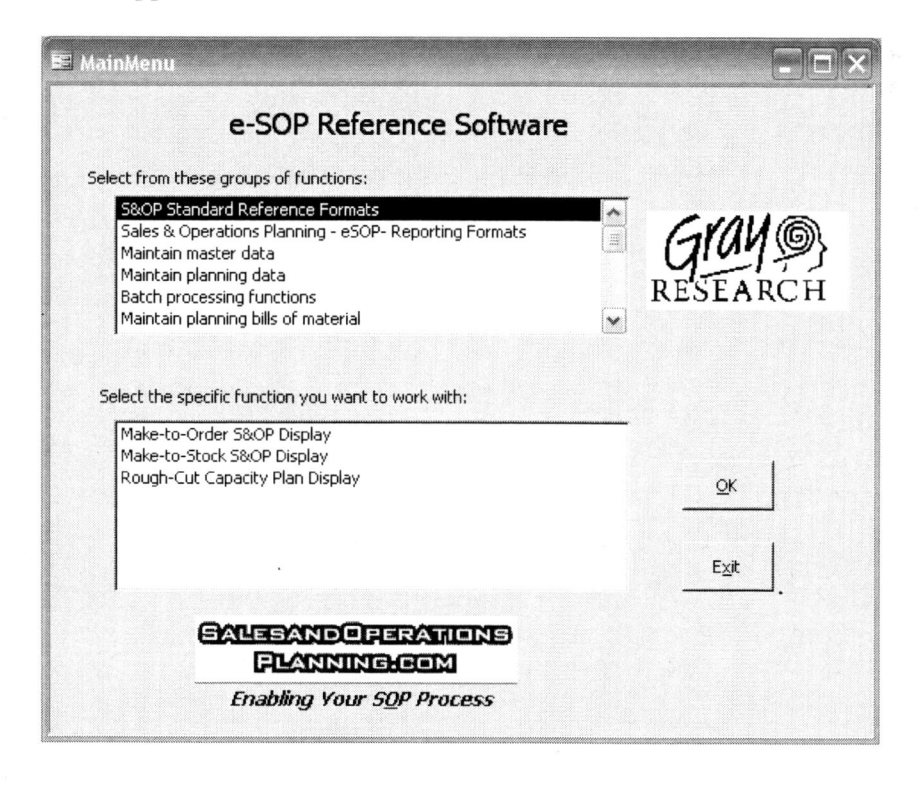

The standard e-SOP user interface provides the following major groupings of functions:

S&OP Standard Reference Formats
Sales & Operations Planning – eSOP – Reporting Formats
Maintain master data
Maintain planning data
Maintain planning bills of material
Maintain capacity data

120 The Sales and Operations Planning Standard System

Batch processing functions
Month end / month start procedures
Miscellaneous
Customize menu

To use this user interface, simply select the group you are interested in from the top part of the display (group selector). Available functions are shown in the lower display (function selector). Select the one you want to work with and click on "OK" – this will launch the selected function.

Basic Functions of e-SOP

Overview: S&OP Standard Reference Formats
Use these functions to access the reference formats for make-to-stock and make-to-order S&OP displays, and for the rough-cut capacity plan display.

Functions in this group:

Make-to-stock S&OP display
Make-to-order S&OP display
Finish-to-order S&OP display
Rough-cut capacity plan display

Overview: Sales & Operations Planning – eSOP – Reporting Formats
Use these functions to access some alternative formats for make-to-stock and make-to-order S&OP displays, and for the rough-cut capacity plan display. These formats include data feeds from the e-SOP database.

Functions in this group:

MTO S&OP display – primary
MTO S&OP display – simulation
MTS S&OP display – primary
MTS S&OP display – simulation
Rough-cut capacity plan display
Sales Plan (forecast) summary worksheet

Additional Menu Functions

The balance of the menu functions are provided to allow you to enter some of your own data and experiment with the calculations in the system.

Overview: Maintain master data group
These functions maintain the basic descriptive data about families, family groups, resources, the calendar, and sales planning assumptions.

Overview: Maintain planning data
Use these functions to maintain all plans (business plan, sales plan, supply plan, scheduled shipments, inventory plan, backlog) for groups of families and as well as capacity data.

Overview: Batch processing functions group
These functions aggregate sales and operations plans into larger groups of families (say for the overall business) and project capacity requirements: The aggregation function can be used to supported a tiered S&OP process where local families summarize into businesses which summarize into corporate business units which summarize into higher level groups, etc.

Overview: Maintain planning bills of material group
These functions update planning bills of material.

Overview: Month end / month start functions group
These functions can be used to enter actual sales, shipments, supply, inventory, and backlog data from the prior month.

Overview: Miscellaneous group
The functions in this group provide some specialized maintenance and correction logic for the system.

Overview: Customize menu group
These functions provide a way to customize the menu structures in the system.

Appendix A
Accessing the Reference Formats

The reference format examples provided in the software and shown throughout the book are:

- Make-to-stock display
- Make-to-order display
- Finish-to-order display
- Rough-cut capacity planning displays

These reference formats can be found in the following spreadsheets:

MTS_format.xls

> FINAL MTS tab shows the make-to-stock sales and operations plan in units
> Profit projection tab shows the make-to-stock profit projection
> Finance $ tab shows the make-to-stock financial projection

MTO_format

> FINAL MTO tab shows make-to-order sales and operations plan in units
> Profit projection tab shows the make-to-order profit projection
> Finance $ tab shows the make-to-order financial projection

FTO_format

> FINAL MTO tab shows make-to-order sales and operations plan in units
> Profit projection tab shows the make-to-order profit projection
> Finance $ tab shows the make-to-order financial projection

Rough_Cut_Formats.xls

> Rough-Cut Plan tab shows the rough-cut capacity plan
> Pegging tab shows the capacity pegging

Accessing the Reference Spreadsheets

You can launch these spreadsheets directly, or you can use the simple menu system in the eSOP software to select and launch them. Please read the

124 The Sales and Operations Planning Standard System

disclaimer in Appendix D before you open the software or install it on your own computer. Opening or installing the software will be interpreted as accepting the terms and conditions of the disclaimer.

If you choose to use the menu system:

1. Launch eSOP. You can do this by double clicking on eSOP.mdb or you can launch Access, select File … Open and then select eSOP.mdb from the c:\eSOP directory.

2. You will see a "splash screen" showing some information about Gray Research and the copyright notice. This will go away after a few seconds and be replaced by the menu system.

3. Select "S&OP Standard Reference Formats" from the upper pane and then select "Make-to-Stock S&OP display" in the lower pane. Click on OK.

This will launch a spreadsheet containing the make-to-stock S&OP format (MTS_format_examples.xls).

4. Select "S&OP Standard Reference Formats" from the upper pane and then select "Make-to-Stock S&OP display" in the lower pane. Click on OK.

This will launch a spreadsheet containing the make-to-order S&OP format (MTO_format_examples.xls).

4. Select "S&OP Standard Reference Formats" from the upper pane and then select "Rough-Cut Capacity Plan" in the lower pane. Click on OK.

This will launch a spreadsheet containing the capacity planning format (Rough_Cut_Formats.xls).

Appendix B
Accessing the Alternate Formats

The e-SOP software includes a set of alternate formats along with the data feeds to populate them. The alternate formats include:

- Basic make-to-stock display
- Simulation make-to-stock display
- Basic make-to-order display
- Simulation make-to-order display
- Rough-cut capacity planning display

These reference formats can be found in the following spreadsheets:

MTS_Standard_eSOP.xls

> Sales and Operations Plan tab shows the make-to-stock sales and operations plan in units, dollars and hours
> Financial Summ Mfg Families tab shows the make-to-stock profit projection

MTS_Simulation_eSOP.xls

> Sales and Operations Plan tab shows the make-to-stock sales and operations plan in units, dollars and hours
> Financial Summ Mfg Families tab shows the make-to-stock profit projection

MTO_Standard_eSOP.xls

> Sales and Operations Plan tab shows make-to-order sales and operations plan in units
> Financial Summ Mfg Families tab shows the make-to-order profit projection

MTO_Simulation_eSOP.xls

> Sales and Operations Plan tab shows the make-to-stock sales and operations plan in units, dollars and hours

Financial Summ Mfg Families tab shows the make-to-stock profit projection

Rough_cut_Standard_eSOP.xls

Capacity Plan tab shows the rough-cut capacity plan
Pegging tab shows the capacity pegging

Different Design Decisions in the Alternate Formats

Besides the fact that these spreadsheets include feeds to stored data, there are several differences in their design when compared to the reference formats. These are:

1. In the reference displays, the inventory and backlog plans for past periods are not stored in the system. The display of the past period inventory plan and the past period actual inventory calculates what the period numbers were based on the current inventory position, planned and actual sales, and planned and actual supply. In the case of the alternate (eSOP) formats, the spreadsheet retrieves the data stored in the eSOP database.

2. In the reference displays, the "Year-to-Date" totals are shown in a column between the end of the current fiscal year and the next fiscal year. In the eSOP displays, these totals are shown at the top of the time phased plans, along with other descriptive data.

3. In the reference displays, the "Budgeted Results" and "Expected Results" are shown in a column between the current year and next year. In the eSOP formats, these budgeted and expected results are shown in the first data column (column B) of the display.

4. The reference displays include only the normal comparisons of sales and supply data. The eSOP displays provide for two simulation displays that will calculate the supply plan from a fixed sales and inventory or sales and backlog plan.

Launching the Spreadsheets

You can launch these spreadsheets directly, or you can use the simple menu system in the eSOP software to select and launch them.

Please read the disclaimer in Appendix D before you open the software or install it on your own computer. Opening or installing the software will be interpreted as accepting the terms and conditions of the disclaimer.

If you choose to use the menu system:

1. Launch eSOP. You can do this by double clicking on eSOP.mdb or you can launch Access, select File ... Open and then select eSOP.mdb from the c:\eSOP directory.

2. You will see a "splash screen" showing some information about Gray Research and the copyright notice. This will go away after a few seconds and be replaced by the menu system.

3. Select "Sales and Operations Planning – eSOP – Reporting Formats" from the upper pane and then select "MTS S&OP display – primary worksheet" in the lower pane. Click on OK.

This will launch a spreadsheet containing the make-to-stock S&OP format (MTS_Standard_eSOP.xls).

4. Select "Sales and Operations Planning – eSOP – Reporting Formats" from the upper pane and then select "MTS S&OP display – simulation worksheet" in the lower pane. Click on OK.

This will launch a spreadsheet containing the make-to-order S&OP format (MTS_Simulation_eSOP.xls). However, instead of calculating the effect on inventory based on sales and supply decisions (as in the normal S&OP display), this worksheet calculates what supply would have to be to support the stated sales and inventory plan.

5. Select "S&OP Standard Reference Formats" from the upper pane and then select "MTO S&OP display – primary worksheet" in the lower pane. Click on OK.

This will launch a spreadsheet containing the make-to-order S&OP format (MTO_Standard_eSOP.xls).

4. Select "Sales and Operations Planning – eSOP – Reporting Formats" from the upper pane and then select "MTO S&OP display – simulation worksheet" in the lower pane. Click OK.

This will launch a spreadsheet containing the make-to-stock S&OP format (MTO_Simulation_eSOP.xls). However, instead of calculating the effect on backlog based on sales and supply decisions (as in the normal S&OP display), this worksheet calculates what supply would have to be to support the stated sales and backlog plan.

4. Select "Sales and Operations Planning – eSOP – Reporting Formats" from the upper pane and then select "RCCP display" in the lower pane. Click on OK.

This will launch a spreadsheet containing the capacity planning format (Rough_cut_Standard_eSOP.xls).

Appendix C
S&OP Reading List

Read these books for additional information on sales and operations planning. For information about ordering check the Gray Research website: www.grayresearch.com/sopbooklist.htm

SALES AND OPERATIONS PLANNING

Sales and Operations Planning - Best Practices. John Dougherty and Chris Gray, Trafford Publishing 2006. Go inside a "baker's dozen" of the world's best S&OP users.

Sales & Operations Planning - The How-to-Handbook. Tom Wallace. T. F. Wallace & Company. Easy to read and understand explanation of this subject - with tips on implementing and operating effectively.

Sales and Operations Planning Handbook. Donald Rice and John J. Civerolo. J. J. Civerolo, Inc. An excellent "starter kit" for implementing and operating Sales and Operations Planning.

Enterprise Sales and Operations Planning. George Palmatier and Colleen Crum. A business novel covering the basics of S&OP.

Orchestrating Success. Dick Ling and Walter Goddard. John Wiley and Sons. The first book on the subject of sales and operations planning from the pioneer in the field (Ling).

RELATED TOPICS

Master Scheduling in the 21st Century. Tom Wallace and Bob Stahl. Accomplishes two important tasks. First it presents the fundamentals of Master Scheduling in a clear, concise, and complete manner. It's simple and easy to understand. Second it explains the relationship between master scheduling and supply chain management, lean manufacturing and efficient consumer response. Foreword and Lean Manufacturing Appendix by Chris Gray.

Sales Forecasting - A New Approach. Tom Wallace and Bob Stahl. How to forecast less, not more; emphasize teamwork, not formulas; focus on process improvement, not forecast "accuracy".

The MRP II Standard System. Chris Gray/Darryl Landvater. John Wiley and Sons. Defines the core functions that must be present in an MRP II system.

Demand Management Best Practices: Process, Principles and Collaboration. Colleen Crum with George Palmatier. A thorough overview of the demand management process.

Focus Forecasting. Bernard Smith. B. T. Smith and Associates. The original book on the subject.

Focus Forecasting and DRP. Bernard Smith. B. T. Smith and Associates. Better than the original: includes new original material and 15 years of additional experience in making Focus Forecasting work.

Master Scheduling. John Proud. John Wiley and Sons. An in-depth work on master production scheduling.

The Oliver Wight ABCD Checklist for Operational Excellence. Oliver Wight Staff. John Wiley and Sons. Detailed Class A Checklist.

Appendix D
Software Disclaimer

e-SOP Sales and Operations Planning
Copyright (C) 1998-2007 Christopher D. Gray, Gray Research. All rights reserved.

Redistribution and use in source and binary forms, with or without modification, are permitted provided that the following conditions are met:

1. Redistributions of source code must retain the above copyright notice, this list of conditions and the following disclaimer.

2. Redistributions in binary form must reproduce the above copyright notice, this list of conditions and the following disclaimer in the documentation and/or other materials provided with the distribution.

THIS SOFTWARE IS PROVIDED BY THE AUTHOR AND CONTRIBUTORS ``AS IS" AND ANY EXPRESS OR IMPLIED WARRANTIES, INCLUDING, BUT NOT LIMITED TO, THE IMPLIED WARRANTIES OF MERCHANTABILITY AND FITNESS FOR A PARTICULAR PURPOSE ARE DISCLAIMED. IN NO EVENT SHALL THE AUTHOR OR CONTRIBUTORS BE LIABLE FOR ANY DIRECT, INDIRECT, INCIDENTAL, SPECIAL, EXEMPLARY, OR CONSEQUENTIAL DAMAGES (INCLUDING, BUT NOT LIMITED TO, PROCUREMENT OF SUBSTITUTE GOODS OR SERVICES; LOSS OF USE, DATA, OR PROFITS; OR BUSINESS INTERRUPTION) HOWEVER CAUSED AND ON ANY THEORY OF LIABILITY, WHETHER IN CONTRACT, STRICT LIABILITY, OR TORT (INCLUDING NEGLIGENCE OR OTHERWISE) ARISING IN ANY WAY OUT OF THE USE OF THIS SOFTWARE, EVEN IF ADVISED OF THE POSSIBILITY OF SUCH DAMAGE.

Index

A

ABCD checklist	130
Aggregation	121

B

Backlog	27, 36, 38, 40, 46, 47, 81, 97
Belt, Bill	i
Best practices	1, ii, iii, ii, vii, xii, xiii, xv, 4, 129, 130, 140
Budgeting	66, 105
Buffo, Tom	i
Business plan	33, 69, 73, 105

C

Calculations	21, 22, 98
Calendar	20
Capacity	60, 62, 63, 93, 117, 124, 126
Capital planning	74
Cash flow	vi, 70
Ciocys, Deborra	i
Civerolo, John	i, xii, 11, 129
Class A	130
Commentary	33, 41, 98
Compromise meeting	11
Converting	44, 48, 49, 50, 97
COPICS	ix
Customer lead time	97
Customer service	75, 106

D

Daily rates	48, 49
Data gathering and review	5
Descriptive information	33
Design philosophies	xv
Dougherty, John	iii, vii, xii, xiii, xv, 4, 129, 140

E

Enterprise resource planning - ERP	vii, ix, x, xi, 22, 140
Executive S&OP meeting	12

F

Family hierarchies   19
Family, families   5, 6, 7, 8, 9, 10, 12, 13, 18, 19, 20, 22, 23, 24, 25, 27, 29, 30, 33, 34, 38, 43, 48, 52, 53, 54, 57, 60, 61, 65, 67, 70, 72, 75, 76, 77, 80, 81, 83, 97, 98, 99, 101, 102, 104, 106, 113, 115, 116, 117, 118, 121, 125, 126
Financial planning   65
Financial reconciliation   68
Finished goods inventory   73
Finish-to-order - FTO   23, 24, 27, 30, 45, 47, 72, 81, 99, 112, 113, 114, 115, 123
Forecasting   53, 129, 130
Forecasts, detailed   52
Functional checklists   ii, v, 97

G

Gips, Jack   i
Graphical displays   ii, v, 28, 87, 90, 107
Gray, Chris   ii, iii, iv, xii, 4, 111, 115, 124, 127, 129, 130, 131, 140

H

Heenan, Phil   i
High/low planning   45, 46, 47
History   26
Horizon   26

I

Inventory   viii, 26, 27, 29, 33, 35, 36, 37, 38, 45, 47, 72, 73, 75, 79, 80, 81, 93, 97, 106
Inventory target   97
Inventory turnover   38
Inventory/backlog plan   29

J

Jones, Bob   i

K

Kasoff, Ron   i
Key performance indicator - KPI   5, 13, 75, 77

L

Landvater, Darryl   ii, iii, ix, xv, 130, 140

Lean manufacturing	129
Lessons learned	iii, i
Ling, Richard	129
Linkages	52
Linking	i, v, 43, 52, 53
Lopker, Pam	ii
Lucas, Eileen	ii

M

Make-to-order - MTO	7, 10, 11, 21, 22, 23, 24, 27, 29, 30, 38, 45, 46, 71, 76, 81, 97, 98, 99, 106, 112, 113, 114, 115, 117, 120, 123, 124, 125, 127, 128
Make-to-stock - MTS	7, 10, 11, 21, 22, 23, 24, 27, 29, 30, 37, 39, 45, 71, 72, 76, 81, 97, 98, 99, 106, 112, 113, 114, 115, 116, 120, 123, 124, 125, 126, 127, 128
Managing change	i, v, 43
Manufacturing resource planning - MRP II	130
Master production scheduling, master scheduling - MPS	v, x, 53, 54, 70, 72, 77, 81, 82, 83, 106, 129, 130
Material requirements planning - MRP	ix, x, 58, 130
Monden, Yasuhiro	x
Monheit, Matty	ii

O

On-time performance	82
Operational takt time	50
Orlicky, Joseph	ix, x
OTIF	75, 78, 79, 106

P

Performance to plan	75, 106
Postponement	32
Pre-S&OP meeting	11
Prevatte, Jim	ii
Prior plans	35, 36
Profit	vi, 69, 75, 79, 106, 123

R

Rabhi, Michel	ii
Reference formats	ii, 115, 119, 120, 123, 124, 127
Reference software	1, iii, ii, v, xii, 111, 112, 119
Reporting	25
Revenue	67, 69, 79
Revenue and profit projections	67, 79
Rice, Don	ii, xii
Rough-cut capacity planning - RCCP	vi, 59, 61, 70, 90, 103, 107, 123, 125, 128
Rough-cut material planning - RCMP	59, 60, 64
Rough-cut planning	57
Routings	59, 61, 102

S

S&OP Basics	i, v, 17
Sales plan	6, 25, 48, 50, 73
Sales planning	6, 25
Sampson, Bob	ii
Schedule stability	77, 82, 106
Shipments	47, 80
Supply	9, 11, 21, 27, 28, 35, 45, 46, 47, 48, 50, 53, 54, 73, 81, 83, 98
Supply chain	vii, viii, xv, 1, 2, 3, 8, 9, 12, 13, 19, 20, 61, 82, 129
Supply plan	9, 11, 28, 35, 45, 46, 47, 48, 50, 53, 54, 73, 81, 83
Supply planning	9, 11

T

Takt time	21, 50
Targets	36
The MRPII Standard System	ii, iii, ix, 140
Time phased data	27, 33, 34, 41, 100, 118

V

Validation	i, v, 43, 44
Visibility	xvi, 35

W

Wallace, Tom	ii, xiii, 129
Weirman, Ken	ii
Wight, Oliver	ix

About the Author

Christopher D. Gray:
Chris Gray has been at the forefront of applying proven manufacturing management methods and concepts for three decades. Since 1979, he has helped more manufacturing and distribution companies resolve resource planning software issues than anyone else in the field. He has been involved in the design and development of both resource planning and lean manufacturing software. His ideas about resource planning software (MRPII and ERP) have influenced the design of nearly every major supplier in the field, and his concepts of how lean manufacturing can be supported by software have been used by the leading supplier of software to the automotive sector to develop a comprehensive lean manufacturing system.

He has written five books:

- The Right Choice, A Complete Guide to Evaluating, Selecting, and Installing MRPII Software, 1987.
- The MRPII Standard System, A Handbook for Manufacturing Software Survival, coauthored with Darryl Landvater, 1989.
- The MRPII Standard System Workbook, co-authored with Darryl Landvater, 1989.
- Sales and Operations Planning - Best Practices, co-authored with John Dougherty, 2006.
- Sales and Operations Planning Standard System, 2007.

Chris is President of Gray Research and one of the founders of Partners For Excellence. Gray Research offers consulting and education on the concepts and methods of world class performance. Partners For Excellence offers counseling and public and private seminars and workshops for executives and managers trying to make the changes needed for improved performance.

Chris was president of Oliver Wight Software Research, Inc. and one of the Oliver Wight Education Associates. During his consulting career, he has been associated with the Oliver Wight Companies, R. D. Garwood, Inc., and Partners for Excellence.

Chris has a BA in mathematics from Washington and Jefferson College and a MS in mathematics from Carnegie Mellon University. He is a past president of the North Shore chapter of APICS and is certified by APICS as a Fellow. He has spoken at numerous international conferences on manufacturing systems and methods. He is listed in six different volumes of Who's Who: Who's Who in America, Who's Who in the East, Who's Who in America's Emerging Leaders, Who's Who in Finance and Industry, Who's Who in Science and Engineering, and Who's Who in the World.

ISBN 142511542-X